SHAKESPEARE'S
POLITICAL
PLAYS

H. M. Richmond

UNIVERSITY OF CALIFORNIA, BERKELEY

Studies in Language and Literature

Shakespeare's
Political
Plays

RANDOM HOUSE · NEW YORK

FIRST PRINTING

© Copyright, 1967, by Random House, Inc.

All rights reserved under International and Pan-American Copyright Conventions. Published in New York by Random House, Inc. and simultaneously in Toronto, Canada, by Random House of Canada Limited

Library of Congress Catalog Card Number: 67–11692

Manufactured in the United States of America by The Colonial Press, Inc., Clinton, Mass.

Typography by Victoria Dudley

For my parents

PREFACE

THIS STUDY does not undertake to supersede any earlier discussions of Shakespeare's history plays. Despite my attempts to re-evaluate certain plays, such as *Richard II, Henry V*, and *Coriolanus*, I do not wish to repudiate the substance of any earlier ingenious interpretations. My experience of Shakespeare's works has convinced me that his prime distinction is his accessibility to any reasonably discriminating premise for judgment. It *is* true, however, that this universality has its roots in a quality that is less uniformly stressed in discussions of his genius than I could wish: his intelligence. Without his extraordinary verbal facility, to be sure, Shakespeare could never have been a great poet; without his unique power of self-projection into the roles of others, he could never have become a great dramatist; but both these resources are functions of an intellect that, like Milton's rather different one, will bear comparison with the best in recorded intellectual history. The fact that his works lend themselves to such diversified exposition may lie less than is sometimes thought in the mere absence of a predetermined personal outlook. His universality probably lies in a deeper logic (although not necessarily an unconscious or intuitive one) than that of many of his critics, whose genius is often far less flexible.

This belief of mine has been strengthened by a sense of

the subtle coherence and endless counterpoint within each of his works, which often governs even the most delicate and widely separated details in a particular play. I have therefore been encouraged to approach each play—as G. Wilson Knight did with the tragedies—as a total unity, a unique "world" of the imagination, whose attributes ensure the meaningfulness of *all* its component parts. In most of these essays, I shall not be content to leave a play without having established some plausible function for all its elements in relation to a central meaning.

This is a large aspiration, and perhaps one impossible to achieve; and it is not intended to suggest that any such coherence is necessarily acceptable to modern taste. The distinction of Shakespeare, like that of Hobbes (whose political philosophy he often seems to prefigure), is that we cannot readily repudiate even what we may dislike in him: the perceptions are too telling and too stringent. Moreover, it appears to me that, far from being an incidental element in our response to the plays as they are performed in an actual theater, this subtle philosophical coherence is actually the key to their fascinating complexity. Only the profoundest intellectual formulations could sustain such conscious dramatic versatility. This we can see by comparing Shakespeare's plays with the more narrowly conceived productions of his contemporaries, Marlowe and Jonson.

I am quite willing to agree that these propositions could be reversed, and that it could be no less plausibly argued that only an exquisitely versatile dramatist, concerned above all to rivet his audience's attention to the stage, could have been moved to fashion so philosophically exciting a combination of intellectual resources. The defect of this aesthetic approach, however, is that it leaves one in the end only with either a magnificent display of technical virtuosity or an artifact whose beauty is an end in itself. I am enough of a puritan and a student to feel that no product of human genius can avoid bearing intelligibly on the effective motives and performance of all men.

Shakespeare seems to me to be a good dramatist at least in part because he is a subtle political philosopher.

His history plays do not merely use historical facts (as they were known to the Elizabethans) to lend color to what are essentially fictions; they deliberately engage in a substantial and steadily evolving study of man as a political animal whose behavior is recorded fact. The facts, then, should be adjusted only locally, to suit the modes and requirements of theatrical performance, and not according to the arbitrary dictates of some pattern of aesthetics. And in his history plays Shakespeare's fidelity to the spirit of his themes has modified, if not codified, certain characteristic attributes of English political consciousness; it is at least partly my concern to trace this process in the following pages. Each essay obviously depends on debts I owe not only to the works listed in the bibliography, but also to numerous individuals with whom I share a fascination with Shakespeare. Not least of them is my wife, whose scholarly expertise in Elizabethan drama has saved me from numerous blunders. Line references to all quotations from Shakespeare are clued to Hardin Craig's collected edition (Scott, Foresman, 1951). The whole project owes its practical realization to the initiative and good will of Mr. David Dushkin.

H. M. R.

Berkeley,
July 1965

CONTENTS

CONTENTS

SHAKESPEARE'S
POLITICAL
PLAYS

INTRODUCTION

DRAMA HAS probably always had its natural origins in religious ritual; this is certainly the case with both classical and modern theater. The Greek drama grew out of choric hymns at religious festivals; and the "tropes," or brief dramatic episodes introduced into the mass on appropriate occasions like Easter or Christmas, provided the germ of those great medieval cycles of biblical playlets that were performed in many English cities. The evolution of the Elizabethan theater from these medieval origins reflects the steady secularization of the tradition—first in the extraction of the tropes from the mass; then in the increased role of the laity, and performances outside the church setting; finally, in the choice of wholly secular subjects. However, the vast sweep of material in the biblical cycles, their indifference to time and place as they moved from the Creation to the Last Judgment, remained a permanent characteristic of the secular theater that evolved from them. Only a few, unhistorical Shakespearean plays, such as *The Comedy of Errors*, *Othello*, and *The Tempest*, show any approximation to the neoclassical unities, whose thematic limitations and rigid decorum are quite alien to the broad, bold, and often disjointed and unpredictable movement of biblical history.

The complications arising from the religious origins of the secular stage were further intensified by inheritances of a positively anti-Christian character from seasonal festivities that still survive today, in nominally Christianized forms, in many of the folk customs of Christmas, the New Year, Spring and Harvest Festivals, and the like. How powerful an influence these ultimately pagan festivities exercised on Elizabethan drama is to be seen in their persistence in so many Shakespearean plays. Allusions to them appear in such titles as *A Midsummer Night's Dream* and *Twelfth Night*, not to mention the harvest masque of *The Tempest*, or the complex woodland rites of which Falstaff is made the victim in *The Merry Wives of Windsor*. Many of the pagan festivals had something of the cathartic function that Aristotle saw in tragedy, although the emotional release they provided characteristically involved comic reversals of values. Figures like the Lord of Misrule and the Boy Bishop usurped authority at prescribed times in the medieval year—in rituals that still survive in modern carnival festivities. Shakespearean characters such as Sir Toby Belch and Falstaff inherit this role of a usurping paganism, which temporarily triumphs over the forces of order and decorum, to the scandal and fear of the sober and the conventional.

But the fusion of these elements in the drama took time; though there are traces of it in the cycle plays, these plays fell progressively into disfavor as new forms and subtler tastes evolved. In the fifteenth century, plays began to appear that were focused on the unifying principle of a single personality—usually of a biblical character, as in the Digby *Mary Magdalen*. While these plays frequently dealt with the life of Christ or of one of his apostles or associates, they also often turned their attention to much later saints—for example, the *Play of Saint Nicholas*. With the advent of the Reformation, even these "miracle" plays became unfashionable, largely because of their Papist associations. They were succeeded in popular favor in England by moralizing dramas that at first followed the medieval literary pattern of allegory—such plays as *The Castle of Perseverance* and *Everyman* (both late fifteenth century),

Mankind, Wit and Science, and others. The vestigial survival of this particular tradition in Elizabethan times is made clear in the structure of *Dr. Faustus,* with its devils, dance of the seven deadly sins, good and bad angels, and so on. It is also apparent in the polarization of Falstaff, as Hal's evil genius in the second part of *Henry IV,* by the staunchly virtuous figure of the Lord Chief Justice—an opposition further reinforced by numerous associations in the text between Falstaff and the vice figures of the moralities with their characteristic trappings (see p. 144).

It is not surprising that the search for concrete examples to confirm the ethical principles of the earlier moralities should have suggested a progression from such tedious abstractions as those of Skelton's political morality, *Magnificence,* to the particularities of, for example, Bishop Bale's *King John.* Bale's choice of subject may have been made the more readily since a play with an historical subject, *King Robert of Sicily,* had already been performed much before his play, in 1529, and had indeed existed long before that time. However, Bale's play is still not really a history play but a violently anti-papal morality, given weight by its historical allusions—and indeed this was the role of English historical writing in general throughout the sixteenth century.

In the previous century, Lydgate's *The Fall of Princes* (derived from Boccaccio's *De Casibus Virorum Illustrium*) had set a kind of norm in utilizing the misfortunes of great men of the past as an admonition to mankind to take heed of the frailty of its hopes in this world (this was along the same lines as Chaucer's *Monk's Tale,* with its dreary list of "tragic" histories). The tradition was powerfully reinforced in the middle of the sixteenth century by *The Mirror for Magistrates,* which ploddingly narrated the moralized biographies of great men and how they had failed, for the edification of their modern equivalents. The drama no less ploddingly reflected this arbitrary view of history in such plays as the first English tragedy, *Gorboduc,* which drew on legendary British history to discuss the question of orderly succession—a theme that had some bearing on the state of the childless Elizabeth, before whom it was first performed.

The allegorical figures have now almost disappeared, and it is clear that interest in political history is acquiring the upper hand over morality, as far as formal structure of meaning is concerned. We can in fact read, in the Venetian ambassador's report home during 1559, of a dramatic performance at court that already aspired to historical plausibility: "And amongst the rest, in one play, they represented King Philip, the late Queen of England, and Cardinal, reasoning together about such things as they imagined might have been said by them in the matter of religion." This suggests something very close to the character of the Shakespearean history play, although it only hints at the range and depth of his later plays. However, it does show how the Tudor anti-papal policy acted as the catalyst for the development of historical awareness, in the effort to review the previous reign of the Catholic Mary Tudor—just as Bale had been driven to look back to King John's defiance of the Pope as a precedent for the policies of Henry VIII.

While the authorities were stringently opposed to any contemporary, not to speak of "subversive" elements in sixteenth-century drama, they did not look with disfavor on plays dealing with political subjects set in the past—particularly if these plays treated their subjects in a manner favoring the Tudor political settlement that had ended England's civil war. One can see this official attitude reflected in such works of criticism as Gosson's *School of Abuse*, which attacks drama as subversive and corrupting, yet favors a play called *Ptolemy*—partly no doubt because it is safely set in the ancient past, but also for "very lively describing how seditious estates with their own devices, false friends with their own swords, and rebellious commons in their own snares, are overthrown." This sort of presentation presumably served to discourage any attempts to dislodge the Tudors on the grounds of their somewhat tenuous claims to the throne. There is no doubt that an earlier Latin play, *Richardus Tertius* (1570), was also intended to contribute to the same effect, by illustrating the Tudor myth of the exceptional viciousness of the last Yorkist king, Richard III, whom the Tudors had killed and dispossessed of his kingdom at the battle of Bosworth Field (1485).

The fact is that the Tudors did achieve a major step forward in historiography, paradoxically enough, by such deliberate furthering of their own political propaganda. Just as Geoffrey of Monmouth had stabilized ancient English history with Norman interests in mind, so the Italian humanist Polydore Vergil was employed to rephrase English history by bringing it into harmony with Tudor policy. The elegant Latin history that he produced marks an important step forward as the first official history of England; it was buttressed by such lesser works as the biography of Richard III, ascribed to Sir Thomas More, in which the monstrous nature of the Tudor's victim was established. Inevitably, while these works favored the Tudors and such English antecedents as could be drawn on to justify their present policies of state, the drama equally reflected their religious and nationalistic views. Thus it fostered the development of English self-awareness, by presenting an image of Englishness through the survey of England's history—happily combining this new didactic role with the more traditional ones of the old morality, miracle, and mystery plays. Thomas Heywood notes in his *Apology for Actors* (1612) that:

Plays have made the ignorant more apprehensive, taught the unlearned the knowledge of many famous histories, instructed such as cannot read in the discovery of all our English chronicles; and what man have you now of that weak capacity that cannot discourse of any notable thing recorded even from William the Conqueror, nay from the landing of Brutus, until this day? being possessed of their true use, for or because plays are writ with this aim, and carried with this method: to teach their subjects obedience to their king; to show the people the untimely ends of such as have moved tumults, commotions, and insurrections; to present the flourishing estate of such as live in obedience, exhorting them to allegiance, dehorting them from all traitorous and fellonious stratagems.

The preferred subjects were obvious enough—Richard III for execration; John (somewhat ironically, to a modern view) as a prototype of English resistance to insidiously Italianate papal dominion and intrigue; Henry V and the Lancastrians as dashing usurpers who had justified their acts by heroic feats of arms in France (which readily suggested analogies, when the failure of the Armada inflicted as humiliating a blow on Spain as Agincourt had been on France). About the time that Shakespeare arrived in London there already existed prototypes for several of his later plays that were to deal with such subjects. *The True Tragedy of Richard the Third*, before getting down to the material that Shakespeare later developed, starts in morality style with an allegorical scene in which Poetry submits to the instructions of Truth (thus foreshadowing the opening of *Henry IV, Part 2*, when Rumour addresses the audience). The two parts of *The Troublesome Reign of John King of England* limit their materials arbitrarily to the quarrels with the Pope and with France, and the plight of Prince Arthur—giving marked prominence, as does Shakespeare in his version, to the role of the Bastard Faulconbridge, who outdoes John in Englishness.

Two of the most interesting of the pre-Shakespearean history plays deal with the fall of Richard II and the career of Henry V. The former was probably a sequence that covered the whole of Richard's reign; of the text, only the first part, *Thomas of Woodstock*, is extant. This selects its materials and utilizes them with more coherence than was shown by *The Troublesome Reign*. It reveals the decay of Richard's kingdom under the corrupting influence of his favorites; and it explains the Lancastrian precedent for the Tudor usurpation. This play, like *The*

Famous Victories of Henry the Fifth, contains many scenes that suggest the disorders centered on Falstaff in Shakespeare's second tetralogy; the two plays do a great deal to provide a rough outline for the material that Shakespeare was later to fill in by a careful study of alternative sources, such as the popular narrative ballads, chronicles of ancient traditions and hearsay, such as John Stow's, and above all the most fruitful of all of Shakespeare's sources, the histories of Edward Hall and Raphael Holinshed.

In many ways the two anonymous plays were Shakespeare's best dramatic prototypes in the genre of the history play, for such a play as Greene's *Scottish History of James IV* is actually no more than a version of an Italian romance of no historical substance, while the historical material in his delightful *Friar Bacon and Friar Bungay* is only a little more substantial. Among recognized dramatists, Peele alone contributed significantly to the genre in the period just before *Henry VI, Part 1*. He drew on the example of Marlowe's *Tamburlaine* to give his own *Edward I* (otherwise a fragmentary and limping drama) more pageantry and colorful staging than was customary. More originally, he also stressed that somewhat aggressive nationalism that colors much of Shakespeare's work. Typical of this vein are the following lines, from the speech of Peele's Queen Mother, which opens his play:

Illustrious England, ancient seat of kings,
Whose chivalry hath royalised thy fame,
That sounding bravely through the terrestrial vale,
Proclaiming conquests, spoils, and victories,
Rings glorious echoes through the farthest world;
What warlike nation, trained in feats of arms,
What barbarous people, stubborn or untamed, . . .
Erst have not quaked and trembled at the name
Of Britain and her mighty conquerors? . . .
Thus Europe, rich and mighty in her kings,
Hath feared brave England, dreadful in her kings.

One readily detects the recurrence of this note in many

parts of Shakespeare's *Henry VI*, and more memorably in John of Gaunt's famous deathbed harangue to the unsympathetic Richard II.

Such are the historical outlines of the development of the Elizabethan history play up to the time of Shakespeare's association with the London theaters, yet these provide, in themselves, only a partial sense of the character of the genre and its potential. The word "history" was used very loosely as a way to describe plays when it first appeared in the court Revels Accounts in 1571. At that time, it was usually used in the sense in which we would now use "story." By 1600, however, there was a large group of plays whose main interest depended on the substantially authentic political history from which they derived their plots and characterizations—an attribute often reinforced by such a phrase as "The True Tragedy" in their title.

Nevertheless, despite such clues and the great popularity of the genre, aesthetically speaking the essential character of the history play is extremely difficult to define. Perhaps the only firm general statement that can be made about it is that it is concerned with events that, for the most part, are generally believed to have actually occurred in the past, although—necessarily—not in the exact pattern presented by the particular play. It is clear that, while such a definition excludes a work like *Othello*, which was derived from a *novella* by the Italian writer Cinthio, and the somewhat similarly derived *Romeo and Juliet*, almost every other serious Shakespeare play is in fact derived from material of an historical character. There was not only a real Julius Caesar and Mark Antony; there was also an historical Macbeth and a Hamlet, not to mention a Cymbeline.

As art aspires to verisimilitude it tends toward such traditional themes of evident substance in recognition of the added force that authentic historical fact may give to imaginative creation. The earliest history play extant is Aeschylus' *The Persians*. It dealt with the Persian invasion of Greece led by Xerxes, a conflict in which Aeschylus himself is supposed to have played a part. Since then, the history play has not flourished in Elizabethan England alone; Schiller, Ibsen, Strindberg, Shaw, and Brecht —to name only a few authors—have all found the force of detailed history an invaluable asset to the imaginative impact of their plays. Yet if an historical theme has become a familiar literary resource, this hardly helps to explain why we distinguish the history play as a genre from tragedy and comedy, just as we distinguish the historical novel from other forms of prose fiction. The deciding factor must lie in the balance that is struck between imaginative and historical elements in a particular play. If, for example, historical facts are given priority over aesthetic considerations (as they are in Shaw's epilogue to *St. Joan*), then presumably we have a history play rather than a tragedy or a comedy—even though the play may, at least approximately, fit into these genres too.

Yet to ask what the consequences are of thus favoring the historical content in a work of art is to imply a conflict between aesthetic discipline and historical fidelity, when there is in fact little justification for such supposed opposition. The historian differs from the less circumstantial artist not in that he eschews any ordering principle of selection and interpretation (he would then be merely a chronicler), but only in the fullness and authenticity of his allusions. Homer is valuable both historically and aesthetically, and a modern historian, such as Gibbon or Toynbee, comes very close to an epic form of statement. The discipline of the history play may then be said to lie in accommodating the medium of drama, with all its requirements of dynamic action and confrontation of characters, to the didactic purpose of presenting the most comprehensive statements of available historical information on the subject that are compatible with the interest of an audience. It may even be said that the simpler (and more exclusive) the aesthetic and philosophical ordering principles adopted by the author, the less authentic, the less historical, as well as the less challenging the play will be.

The history play, then, is precariously balanced as a genre—between falsification of fact in the interest of entertainment or propaganda, and the crushing of interest by the mere conscientious accumulation of factual detail. The best history plays will be plausible and exciting—but they will almost necessarily be aesthetically unorthodox and not conventionally interpretable. They will risk being blamed (as the pre-Shakespearean plays have been) for arbitrariness, lack of focus, and inconsistency, and the author's attempt to avoid these criticisms may propel him into falsification and simplification of his material—which will invite no less censure.

In practice, the character of many of the plays written within the genre of the "history" may hardly seem to justify much rigor of definition. The Elizabethan audience in particular was apparently not interested in aesthetic principles, so much as in information about its native land, in enthusiastic presentation of its past triumphs, and in a suitable employment of vivid episodes or sharp confrontations. In reading Shakespeare's history plays one must therefore recall that for an English audience, even today, many of the figures and events presented have an intrinsic resonance and an automatic claim on their attention, independent of any aesthetic considerations. Numberless insignificant and incidental associations perpetually catch at the attention of an English audience; they are an intrinsic part of the entertaining yet eminently didactic functioning of the history play as the Elizabethans knew it.

There is no doubt that Shakespeare's two great tetralogies as well as the four or five other plays of his that are derived from English history begin to approach an epic statement of English experience—as influential on Englishmen and their political self-awareness as Homer was on that of the Greeks. That Shakespeare was aware of this impact we shall see above all in *Henry V*, and it is a consideration that renders more complex the critic's response to this and the other plays, because it adds yet another level to an analysis of their function. They are not only didactic in the sense of communicating information and establishing moral perspectives in the tradition of the medieval drama; they are also, under the impetus of Tudor policies, calculatedly political in very much the same way as Hobbes is in his *Leviathan*, or Burke in his *Reflections on the French Revolution*. Shakespeare would have been an anomaly in his time if he had failed consciously to pursue these considerations in framing his plays.

Shakespeare's own complex response to his material was further defined by a variety of more narrowly biographical characteristics. Although he was well educated, his origins were provincial and middle-class, and he was less committed to the cosmopolitan formality of the typical university graduates (like Marlowe) and courtiers (like Sidney), who dominated the literature of the time. It is striking that the two most powerfully sustained literary careers of this period—those of Jonson and Shakespeare—both show a unique response to experience, derived from this lack of full conditioning to the traditional academic or social responses. Jonson lost his father early, and though he also received a good preliminary education at Westminster School in London, his stepfather even apprenticed him as a bricklayer for a time. Shakespeare's background was even more complex. His father's career was erratic: it took him to the head of the Stratford local administration, yet also involved him in a variety of legal difficulties that began with his first entry onto the pages of history, when he was fined for keeping an illegal dunghill in a Stratford street. Financial troubles seem to have plagued the father's old age—and he was fined for failure to attend church, either avoiding his creditors thereby, or showing traces of recusant Catholic hostility toward the new, Tudor-founded Church of England (Shakespeare's daughter Susanna was later also cited for nonattendance).

Shakespeare's own personal life was equally full of complexities—at the age of eighteen, he married a woman who was seven years older than himself, and the marriage was both incorrectly recorded and took place away from the bride's home. A child was born too soon after the ceremony and, not so very long after, Shakespeare left this family (now increased by twins) under rather enigmatic circumstances—legend providing various ingenious explanations for his departure and what he did during the following few years. His reappearance in London associated him with the highest society in the land; he now showed an extraordinary sophistication and refinement, which betrayed him into further complex relationships, both with the young man and with the Dark Lady who figure prominently in the Sonnets. Later on he was bound over to keep the peace, by some enemy whom he had managed to terrify to the point of fearing physical violence. He appears to have lived with a French Huguenot family in London, which provided him with yet another exceptional perspective on national values.

Even his daughter Judith seems to have sustained the family's somewhat erratic traditions. Not only was her overhasty marriage in 1616 followed by the excommunication of both of the newlyweds, but it soon proved that she had managed to choose her spouse even more awkwardly than her father had, for soon after Judith was married to Mr. Thomas Quiney, Shakespeare rewrote his will, to Quiney's disadvantage. His reasons were revealed six weeks after the marriage, when the records show that Quiney was publicly censured for adultery with one Margaret Wheeler. It is somewhat shocking to learn that the Stratford parish register declares that Margaret and Quiney's illegitimate child were buried one month after Quiney's marriage to Judith Shakespeare.

The Shakespeare family was thus perhaps more than usually susceptible to difficulties and even disasters, such as the premature death of the poet's only son, Hamnet, in 1596, at the age of eleven. Certainly it is the sort of background that would condition the playwright against presenting life in his plays in terms of confident simplicity, basing itself on elementary moral, social, or political views. It can thus be argued that the life of Shakespeare, the theatrical genre he favored, and the political and ecclesiastical situation of the time, conspired to produce a series of plays of the most complex structure—moralizing, yet emotionally multidimensional; politically alert, yet skeptical of facile solutions; traditional in form, but uniquely subtle in both texture and structure.

I

THE FIRST TETRALOGY

I

Henry VI
Part One

IN *Henry VI*, despite the appearance of King Henry in all three parts, there are no central personal relationships of the kind that define other tragic drama. The focus shifts freely from Gloucester to Talbot, to Joan, to the King and so on, in a seemingly endless series of juxtapositions. The work thereby defies Aristotelian aesthetics of the kind that is so characteristic of post-medieval European writing, in which overt structure and consistency are highly prized. Modern drama, for example, affords almost no parallels to the *Henry VI* series, whose norms belong rather to a literary tradition that was nearing its end when this series was written. This is the medieval tradition of the multiple narrative, which is best compared —if to any classical genre—to that of the Hesiodic epic. Such a vast, irregular type of structure has always been profoundly attractive to English authors, in contrast to the disciplined aesthetics of most classical writing, and the more recent norms of the Romance literatures. *The Canterbury Tales* is one example of this peculiarly English vein; it blends a series of locally unified narratives of a highly refined character into a complex interplay of literary patterns whose intent is uncertain, although the effect is peculiarly evocative and critically stimulating. This nominal incompleteness may remind us of a later, similarly incomplete and highly episodic poem written just before *Henry VI—The Faerie Queene*—which nostalgically revived the style of the medieval romances, and in part echoed Malory's *Morte d'Arthur*.

It is, however, in Chaucer's contemporary, Langland, that the peculiar difficulty and subtlety of the multiple structure appears most strikingly. At first, *Piers Ploughman* seems to lack all coherence, to be a kind of epic medley of thoughts on religious matters, shot through with episodic narratives and fluctuating allegories. In the end, however, the work tends to establish a world that is even more doctrinally and socially varied than that created by the aesthetically more refined, yet temperamentally more elusive genius of Chaucer. Langland defines his complex theological terms not by sustained formal patterns but by the apparently random accumulation of associations. Through a seemingly aimless series of juxtapositions, he creates an imaginative environment whose authenticity and force derive in part from its presentation in terms that appear to be as arbitrary as those of the real world. Such juxtapositions offer no facile—albeit reassuring—coherence. Only with such works as Proust's vast sequence, or in the rambling structure of Ezra Pound's *Cantos*, can we find a modern analogy—these works seem to reach out to new patterns with their own complex and comprehensive themes, philosophies, and judgments of experience. It is by such a work that we are confronted in the three parts of *Henry VI*.

If this is so, then it is not enough to dismiss the plays as so confused as to be necessarily the work of an ill-assorted team of co-authors, even if there are some grounds for linking them (at least for their sources or models) with Greene, Marlowe, and Peele, as well as with Shakespeare. Nor can we deal with the plays in terms of the problems involved in a naive chronicle of national history: the tone is too harsh to suit local patriotism. While the plays often appear to be made up of arbitrarily chosen episodes from the fifty-year reign of Henry VI, one can still strongly sense the unique cumulative effect that these scenes have in reading, not to speak of performance. The critic's real need is to determine whether this effect is of a memorable and significant kind; for the result of such complex literary and social combinations is not necessarily fragmentary, even if its genesis does defy neat explanation. It may display that unity, larger than the perspective of a single author or principle, which is sometimes seen in Homer. We do find an argument in favor of a single author, however, when we recognize in the three parts of *Henry VI* an important move toward the contrapuntal complexity of the later Shakespearean history play.

As for the memorableness of the first part, of that there can be no doubt. The play contains a galaxy of brilliant scenes, beginning with the elegiac opening, through which the death of Henry V dominates the characters and plot. This stroke of literary strategy definitively establishes the gloomy medieval rhythm of the wheel of fortune which destroys both the English hero Talbot and his enemy Joan of Arc, and governs all the plots of the tetralogy. This first disastrous setback to English leadership in the wars with France leads naturally to the discussion of various aspects of the nature of military and political efficiency in the state. The theme provides us with a first glimpse of the implicit statement about the instability of public life of which the action of the plays is the correlative.

It is the essence of the history play (as opposed to narrative history) to present by epitome—to intensify confrontations and polarize issues. In *Henry VI, Part 1*, this process is typified by the brilliantly improvised scene in the Temple Garden (II.iv.). Here the factionalism that progressively undermines Henry V's achievement of a unified and aggressive England is heraldically epitomized through the plucking of red and white roses by the factions of York and Lancaster—a scene for which there was no precedent in history. The abuse of humane reason in this vivid confrontation is carefully stressed. After agreeing to a trial by vote of the issue (itself so incidental as never to be established), both factions fail to maintain decorum. The outcome of the reasonable idea of a vote thus merely intensifies the acerbity of the quarrel.

In the previous scene, by profoundly appropriate juxtaposition, there had also appeared in the conduct of the representative of the best among the English, the elder Talbot, a seemingly no less gross surrendering of his faculties of judgment to facile emotion, aroused by the charms of a French patriot, the seductive Countess of Auvergne. She, like St. Joan, anticipates that fatal energy that so many of Shakespeare's tragic women display. But while Talbot's instincts in the presence of the seductive French Countess also appear to be submerging his reasoning powers, the conclusion of the scene achieves a dramatic reversal, in which he reveals that he has anticipated and neutralized the Countess' emotional strategy. The irony lies in the contrast within each of these two scenes— Talbot appears naive, yet proves discreet, and even ultimately gallant; the factions affect polite and rational debate, yet proceed rapidly to insults and physical threats.

From this particular sequence, it is easy to move out into the larger patterns of the play. The sexual axis of Talbot and the Countess is of the greatest relevance to the recurring rhythms both of this play and of the tetralogy that it introduces. We later find Talbot, for example, confronted by another female representative of the subtle, even diabolical wiles of the French—deceits that Shakespeare characteristically associates with women (even the best of them, such as Viola, Rosalind, and Portia, exploit disguise extravagantly and often quite sadistically). Joan appears to epitomize such traits in this play—she captures Rouen through a disguise that so offends Talbot's sense of decorum that he calls it "treason." Of course, the play takes here, as generally, an anti-French view of Joan. It seems naive, however, to be indignant now over the harshness of the portrait. To expect any Protestant Elizabethan to show a French Catholic heroine as advised not by devils but by angels, so soon after the massacre of St. Bartholomew's day, would be the equivalent of showing in our own post-war years that, say, Bismarck had been similarly well-advised. Furthermore, the play passes a far less contemptuous judgment on Joan's actions than it does on most of the failings of the English representatives—as, for example, on the cowardice of Fastolfe (historically, a mistaken accusation), or the factious dilatoriness of Somerset and York:

> The fraud of England, not the force of France
> Hath now entrapp'd the noble-minded Talbot.
> (IV.iv.36–7)

Yet even this contrast provides an inadequate conclusion about the status of Joan. The play is "against" Joan in much the same way as Aeschylus is against the Persians or Clytemnestra. Just as the Greek author had censured Clytemnestra while still making her a dominating and even heroic figure in the *Oresteia*, so Shakespeare's figure of Joan displays heroic power—even something of the magnetism that the real Joan undoubtedly possessed—and Talbot is made to recognize his weakness in confronting such a figure:

> My thoughts are whirled like a potter's wheel.
> I know not where I am, nor what I do:
> A witch, by fear, not force, like Hannibal,
> Drives back our troops and conquers as she lists.
> (I.v.19–22)

No audience can be insensitive to the energy and passion of this Joan, nor to her subtlety and finesse, which a nominal shift in perspective could readily convert into saintly insight. Her speech to the wavering Burgundy is masterly in its emphasis and emotional strategy:

> Look on thy country, look on fertile France,
> And see the cities and the towns defaced
> By wasting ruin of the cruel foe.
> As looks the mother on her lowly babe
> When death doth close his tender dying eyes,

See, see the pining malady of France;
Behold the wounds, the most unnatural wounds,
Which thou thyself hast given her woeful breast.
O, turn thy edged sword another way;
Strike those that hurt, and hurt not those that help.
                                    (III.iii.44-53)

Joan can strike as true a chord as this—and her power to do so is as much explained as degraded by her final acid comment on the reversed allegiance of the vacillating Burgundy in *Henry VI:* "Done like a Frenchman: turn, and turn again!" Modern tastes cannot calmly confront so skeptical a patriot as this, who succeeds because she is one of those

That do not do the thing they most do show,
Who, moving others, are themselves as stone,
Unmoved, cold, and to temptation slow, . . .
                              (*Sonnet 94, 2-4*)

Yet, by the time he wrote this sonnet, Shakespeare had come to see that history and even Providence are on the side of such people:

They rightly do inherit heaven's graces
And husband nature's riches from expense;
They are the lords and owners of their faces,
Others but stewards of their excellence.
                              (*Sonnet 94, 5-8*)

And Henry V and Octavius Caesar triumph in Shakespeare's writings because in them he carries forward this capacity for plausible rhetoric that he had first assigned to the St. Joan of *Henry VI*.

This element in the portrait of Joan has, of course, no foundations in the Joan of history and the records of her trial, but that incredible person defies literary imagination and has only the authority of fact to support her. As Aristotle observed, drama should be more concerned with what is probable than with that which is merely possible. Joan as she appears in *Henry VI* is frightening rather than noble, but her superhuman effectiveness is very plausible and altogether memorable. Her savage resolution as her army fails (V.ii.1ff.) is as monumental as Lady Macbeth's when faced with the risk of her husband's failure. Joan's confrontation with her father after her capture and her shifts and turns to escape execution are full of an intense energy and love of life that display that potency of Shakespeare's women from which, in part, Shaw developed his theory of the alliance between women and the life force.

One feels indeed the emergence of a plausible interpretation of that almost irresistible determination which had enabled Joan of Arc to transform the military situation in France. The play needs no apology as drama for having substituted near-Machiavellian insight (a far more plausible resource) for the naive faith that, almost incredibly, carried the historical St. Joan so far. And the play does give Joan the last word—one that resonates down to the horrible deaths of York and his family in *Part 3* and beyond. York's dismissal of Joan to death provokes her dying curse, which has the prophetic authority that Shakespeare always gives to those who are soon to die:

> Then lead me hence; with whom I leave my curse:
> May never glorious sun reflex his beams
> Upon the country where you make abode;
> But darkness and the gloomy shade of death
> Environ you, till mischief and despair
> Drive you to break your necks or hang yourselves!
> (V.iv.86–91)

Another brilliant stroke of juxtaposition occurs in the scene between Joan's capture and her final condemnation, a scene that takes us back again to that theme of female duplicity and of women's power as catalysts of evil which was raised by Talbot's confrontation with the Countess of Auvergne. Talbot established the norm of heroic response to such a challenge, yet in the climactic scenes of the play we see how a weaker man introduces into the heart of England a woman who is to sap its inner vitality as effectively as Joan has managed to impair its outward expression. England loses one dangerous enemy at the very moment when its own weakness creates another. Suffolk's responses to his fair French prisoner, Margaret, deserve our closest scrutiny, because here too a great theme of the histories and of Shakespeare's work in general achieves its first, paradoxical formulation. It is in Romeo's terms that Suffolk greets his prize:

> O fairest beauty, do not fear nor fly!
> For I will touch thee but with reverent hands;
> I kiss these fingers for eternal peace,
> And lay them gently on thy tender side.
> Who art thou? say, that I may honour thee.
> (V.iii.46–50)

Margaret, like Juliet, Rosalind, Isabella, and other Shakespearean women when they are confronted by love, strengthens her self-possession in proportion as her admirer loses it. Her cool poise seems to unnerve Suffolk, who sinks into dithering confusion:

> Be not offended, nature's miracle,
> Thou art allotted to be ta'en by me:
> So doth the swan her downy cygnets save,
> Keeping them prisoner underneath her wings.
> Yet, if this servile usage once offend,
> Go and be free again as Suffolk's friend. [*She is going*]
> O stay! [*aside:*] I have no power to let her pass;
> My hand would free her, but my heart says no.
> As plays the sun upon the glassy streams,
> Twinkling another counterfeited beam,
> So seems this gorgeous beauty to mine eyes.
> Fain would I woo her, yet I dare not speak.
> (V.iii.54–65)

The cause of such abruptly flowering love, wherever it appears in Shakespeare, makes it all the more dangerous in a political context—for Shakespeare sees romantic love as essentially the outcome of an attraction between opposites, incompatibles, and those to whom such attraction is forbidden. Thus Romeo loves Juliet, daughter of his family's enemy; the fair Venetian Desdemona loves the dark Moor Othello; the married Roman Antony abandons his obligations in order to pursue the exotic and corrupt Egyptian Cleopatra. Suffolk is similarly attracted to his fair enemy—perhaps the more so because he himself is already married. Indeed, following the classic tradition of occidental romances, Suffolk at once seeks to duplicate the situation of Launcelot, and more particularly of Tristram. The obstacle that gives such love its most exciting dimension is that which confronted the troubadours, who courted the wife of their feudal lord. Tristram delivers his love, Isolde, to his king, Mark, as wife—and Suffolk's conventional sentiments dictate a similar solution, "so my fancy may be satisfied" (V.iii.91). Suffolk consciously plans to unnerve the English, by corrupting them with his own facile enthusiasms. After embracing Margaret (on the king's behalf . . .), he meditates:

> O, wert thou for myself! But, Suffolk, stay;
> Thou mayst not wander in that labyrinth;
> There Minotaurs and ugly treasons lurk.
> Solicit Henry with her wondrous praise:
> Bethink thee on her virtues that surmount,
> And natural graces that extinguish art;
> Repeat their semblance often on the seas,
> That when thou comest to kneel at Henry's feet,
> Thou mayst bereave him of his wits with wonder.
> (V.iii.187–95)

The play significantly concludes with Suffolk making speeches to King Henry in the high sentimental style of Troilus defending the abduction of Helen in Shakespeare's later play, *Troilus and Cressida*. Faced with the practical disadvantages of the marriage of Margaret and Henry, Suffolk makes a rhetorical defense:

> A dower, my lords! disgrace not so your king,
> That he should be so abject, base and poor,
> To choose for wealth and not for perfect love.
> (V.v.48–50)

The vehemence of his exposition successfully unbalances the youthful king. Henry's acceptance of Suffolk's advice brings the action of the play to a close in a speech in which the king reveals an ominous susceptibility to emotion—in striking contrast to Talbot's response to the charms of the Countess of Auvergne:

> Whether it be through force of your report,
> My noble Lord of Suffolk, or for that
> My tender youth was never yet attaint
> With any passion of inflaming love,
> I cannot tell; but this I am assured,
> I feel such sharp dissension in my breast,
> Such fierce alarums both of hope and fear,
> As I am sick with workings of my thoughts.
>   (V.v.79–86)

The very last lines of the play are Suffolk's, as he gloats with satisfaction over the triumph of his self-indulgence, both emotional and political. It is characteristic of Shakespeare that these lines should be forebodingly colored by imagery taken from the classic theme of love-born disaster, the fall of Troy:

> Thus Suffolk hath prevail'd; and thus he goes,
> As did the youthful Paris once to Greece,
> With hope to find the like event in love,
> But prosper better than the Trojan did.
> Margaret shall now be queen, and rule the king;
> But I will rule both her, the king and realm.
>   (V.v.103–8)

Suffolk scarcely understands his own limitations and resources, and his expectations have more than a hint of what the Greeks called *hubris* in them. Margaret is no mean woman and his simple scheme of operation scarcely takes into account his declared estimate of her capacity— which the following plays amply justify—as "a lady of so high resolve" who displays

Her valiant courage and undaunted spirit,
More than in women commonly is seen.
(V.v.70–1)

The play thus ends on a note of pessimism, foretelling
the continuation of those suicidal antagonisms of the English nobility that are to reach their climax in the ensuing
civil wars. But *Henry VI, Part 1* has already mapped out
the latent tensions of a weak body politic. Many men like
Suffolk are waiting the opportunity to turn occasion to
their own profit. The note of ambition is struck in the
very first scene of the play by the Bishop of Winchester,
whose parting lines at the end of that scene smack of the
old moralities in their extravagant monomania:

Each hath his place and functions to attend:
I am left out; for me nothing remains.
But long I will not be Jack out of office:
The king from Eltham I intend to steal
And sit at chiefest stern of public weal.
(I.i.173–7)

This sounds like some figure of crude ambition in a
political morality; throughout the first scene, the Bishop
illustrates the clerical exploitation of political advantage,
of which the Elizabethans no doubt saw the conspicuous
English illustration in a Cardinal of their own century—
Wolsey. The role of Duke Humphrey of Gloucester in
this opening scene is to voice that opposition to such
clerical pretension which every Englishman of Elizabeth's
day would naturally favor, as he indignantly repudiates
the bishop's claims to have won the favor of God for
Henry V by means of the church's prayers:

The Church! where is it? Had not churchmen pray'd
His thread of life had not so soon decay'd:
None do you like but an effeminate prince,
Whom, like a school-boy, you may over-awe.
(I.i.33–6)

This is a home thrust, in view of Winchester's plans to dominate Henry which are revealed at the end of the scene. But Shakespeare never eases dramatic tension by elementary favoritism toward one side, and Gloucester's stridency provokes a shrewd blow in return:

> Thy wife is proud; she holdeth thee in awe,
> More than God or religious churchmen may.
> (I.i.39–40)

Across this kind of needling Bedford cuts sharply, invoking the spirit of the dead Henry V, only to be interrupted himself by a messenger bearing disastrous news, in the style of classical drama:

> Guienne, Champagne, Rheims, Orleans,
> Paris, Guysors, Poictiers, are all quite lost.
> (I.i.60–1)

Shakespeare rapidly achieves a metamorphosis of the messenger to chorus, a role that the tradition of the morality play fosters; for the Elizabethan theater—far from eschewing overt judgment in the modern style—depended for its impact to a large extent on the force of high moral judgments, which carried the full weight of the medieval absolutism and sense of prescribed social function. When he is asked to explain the treachery that had occasioned the losses in France, the messenger replies unequivocally, and quite out of character for such a mere commoner (his very name is omitted):

> No treachery; but want of men and money.
> Amongst the soldiers this is muttered,
> That here you maintain several factions,
> And whilst a field should be dispatched and fought,
> You are disputing of your generals; . . .
> Awake, awake, English nobility!
> Let not sloth dim your honours new-begot.
> (I.i.69–73,78–9)

Successive messengers then drive home the point with (to modern taste) sledge-hammer thoroughness, and the figure of Sir John Fastolfe is finally introduced, as the epitome of the aristocratic sloth and cowardice that here hinders and ultimately destroys its opposite, the heroic Talbot. The actual Sir John was by no means the figure he appears in the play, but a tough and competent soldier who grew old in the Lancastrians' service. Only one actual withdrawal provides even an excuse for the play's judgment on him; but here is an example of that rephrasing of incidental details of history, in the interest of dramatic point and clarity, which the genre of the history play calls for. Of the vicious egoism of the English aristocracy in general in this period, there can be no question. Only Talbot loyally holds his own in France, and that precariously, until (as his enemy Charles testifies) he meets his death—primarily because of the indifference of the English aristocracy:

> Had York and Somerset brought rescue in
> We should have found a bloody day of this.
> (IV.vii.33–4)

This scene on the battlefield where Talbot and his son lie slaughtered gives due honor to the French, whose dignity and maturity are amply borne out in their subsequent behavior. After a suggestion of the Bastard of Orleans that the body of Talbot be disfigured, Charles sharply intervenes:

> O, no, forbear! for that which we have fled
> During the life, let us not wrong it dead.
> (IV.vii.49–50)

Far more memorable is the confrontation of values when, later in the scene, Sir William Lucy seeks an exchange of prisoners—and, believing Talbot to be one of them, devotes a dozen pompous lines to Talbot's titles and honors. Joan replies tersely and contemptuously, ending with two magnificently savage lines:

> Here is a silly stately style indeed!
> The Turk, that two and fifty kingdoms hath

Writes not so tedious a style as this.
Him that thou magnifiest with all these titles
Stinking and fly-blown lies here at our feet.

(IV.vii.72-6)

The tough precision of that last realistic line is hard to
match in the English scenes, and it further vindicates the
supremacy that Joan achieves. The English for the most
part fail to cut through the verbiage and false rhetoric
that their shallow egotism proposes to them. Decisive,
heroic action is beyond them, while Joan, however sinister
her resources and her outlook, shows the same ability to
reshape the basic situation as does the gangster-like Achilles of *Troilus and Cressida*, whose murder of Hector shatters all Trojan hope of victory.

At the heart of the failure of the English to achieve
such ruthless efficiency stands Henry VI himself. His
character and situation are the key to the whole tetralogy
—and the play may seem to go almost extravagantly out
of its way in order to clarify the dynastic situation, if we
do not remember that, no matter how insignificant Henry
may seem at first, he is the pivot on which the action
turns. This is the reason for the long expository scene in
the Tower between Mortimer and his gaolers, and later
with Richard Plantagenet (II.v.). The scene establishes a
fascinating contrast between the two branches of the
Plantagenet family—the usurping Lancastrians, and the
Yorkists who claim the right of true succession to the
throne. The Lancastrians begin as brilliant and calculating
opportunists who are vindicated by their very success. The
dying Mortimer has no illusions about the immediate value
of the claim to the deposed Richard's crown, which he
bequeaths to Richard Plantagenet:

With silence, nephew, be thou politic:
Strong-fixed is the house of Lancaster
And like a mountain, not to be removed.

(II.v.101-3)

But Henry VI is of a different temper from his father and grandfather, as his surrender to Suffolk's romanticism at the end of the play makes clear in a different respect. While his title to the throne is not unquestionable, yet no one would dare to challenge his grip on the sceptre—as long as it is a firm one. It is not.

Several threads of the play knot dangerously at the same point, Act III, Scene i, as a result of the king's inadequacy. In the presence of the king, Gloucester launches into a speech denouncing that "presumptuous priest," the Bishop of Winchester, in terms that would be more suitable to a Reformation anti-clericalist. The distressed Henry knows the political insights of his ancestors only as lessons learned by rote:

> Believe me, lords, my tender years can tell
> Civil dissention is a viperous worm
> That gnaws the bowels of the commonwealth.
> (III.i.71-3)

It is not surprising that this tone fails to quell a fight that breaks out among the retainers, nor does Henry's naively pious address move the Bishop:

> O, how this discord doth afflict my soul!
> Can you, my Lord of Winchester, behold
> My sighs and tears and will not once relent?
> Who should be pitiful, if you be not?
> (III.i.106-9)

Henry is here using emotion, not political argument; he mistakes attitudes for realities, and he is the only one who fails to realize that the truce that is patched up when Gloucester yields is meaningless.

Exeter crudely summarizes these facts as chorus at the end of this scene, and in a later one ruefully notes:

> 'Tis much when sceptres are in children's hands.
> (IV.i.192)

Henry is then not entirely responsible for his inefficiency, but politics shows no respect for causes. Henry is a weak king in that he is, like Othello:

> . . . of a free and open nature,
> That thinks men honest that but seem to be so.
> (*Othello*, I.iii.405–6)

Just as the very innocence of Othello's mind exposes him all the more fully to the rationalized promptings of evil, in the form of Iago, so it is Henry's impulsive desire to resolve a political issue by a consistent and appealing emotional attitude that is ultimately fatal to the stability and well-being of England. In the very scene after that in which Mortimer and Richard had both analyzed their claims to Henry's throne, Henry innocently restores to Richard the high title of Duke of York, suppressed on the execution of Richard's father for treason. Worse, he gives substance to this ominous title that his father Henry V had firmly kept vacant, by adding,

> . . . all the whole inheritance I give
> That doth belong unto the house of York.
> (III.i.164–5)

Thus we are confronted with a king who takes satisfaction in making the gestures of royalty, but remains unaware of the substructure of political mastery which must underlie the grand act, if it is to achieve anything of permanent value. Again and again Henry strikes the high moral note, as when he banishes Fastolfe for his cowardice, or reproaches two quarreling English knights for failing to

> . . . remember where we are;
> In France among a fickle wavering nation:
> If they perceive dissension in our looks
> And that within ourselves we disagree,
> How will their grudging stomachs be provoked
> To wilful disobedience, and rebel! . . .

And therefore, as we hither came in peace,
So let us still continue peace and love.
(IV.i.137–42,160–1)

Yet no sooner has Henry elected himself umpire than he
declares his partiality for the side opposite to that favored
by Richard Duke of York, by assuming the red rose, to
York's irritation. To compound his lack of discretion,
Henry then confers on the silent York the regency of
France, giving power to the man he has just insulted.

Exeter, chorus once again, comments drily on York's
silence under the circumstances:

Well didst thou, Richard, to suppress thy voice;
For, had the passions of thy heart burst out,
I fear we should have seen deciphered there
More rancorous spite, more furious-raging broils,
Than yet can be imagined or supposed.
(IV.i.182–6)

This restraint contrasts with the king's facile rhetoric
which had already been pointed out by an almost condescending comment from Warwick:

My lord of York, I promise you, the king
Prettily, methought, did play the orator.
(IV.i.174–5)

And when York laconically notes that the king has in fact
favored his enemies, Warwick continues:

Tush, that was but his fancy, blame him not;
I dare presume, sweet prince, he thought no harm.
(IV.i.178–9)

York bites back his reply, and the contrast is fully established: the king is facile, and lacks intensity, insight, and
finesse; York, on the other hand, is oblique, tenacious,
ambitious. At one and the same moment, Henry's behavior
both encourages specious rhetoric of the kind that Suffolk
favors and provokes such covert forces as York's resentful

ambition, which can lurk all the more readily in the cover that is provided by the thickets of the king's oratory.

The contrast is not only between Henry and York, however; it is also between Henry and Joan. Confronted with proposals for peace and marriage in France, Henry shows a deplorable lack of initiative:

> Marriage, uncle! alas, my years are young!
> And fitter is my study and my books
> Than wanton dalliance with a paramour.
> Yet call the ambassadors; and as you please,
> So let them have their answers every one.
>
> (V.i.21–5)

The later treaty-breaking surrender by the king to Suffolk's rhetorical advocacy of Margaret follows plausibly upon this weak assent. It is by no accidental contrast that Joan, in the very next scene, fiercely advises the hesitant Charles:

> Of all base passions, fear is most accursed.
> Command the conquest, Charles, it shall be thine,
> Let Henry fret and all the world repine.
>
> (V.ii.18–20)

Joan is sure that he who seizes the moment wins, and in proportion to his own energetic resolution. Henry conspicuously lacks her authority, so that his kingdom disintegrates in proportion as his own flaccid good nature allows Winchester to pursue his relentless vendetta against Gloucester and permits York's hostility to gain momentum.

It now becomes clear that the play has a genuine thematic unity. But it is a subtle and substantial one, based on a complex interaction of ethics and politics, and not merely a formal aesthetic organization. Joan embodies all those dangerous resources and that virile energy that the effeminate Henry lacks; in this, she is paradoxically closer to the practical character of the true saint than is the amiable and mystical Henry whom she opposes. The French are conscious masters of those elusive manipulations that dominate circumstance, while still playing deceptively on the rhetoric of emotion that Henry mistakes for political reality. And just as the English lose their mastery in France because, with the exception of Talbot, they lack this sleight of mind, so at home their country drifts into ruin as these devices are used increasingly there—not to buttress, but to subvert established authority.

The strength of the play lies almost entirely in the plot's vigorous exposition of these political issues, for its style rarely rises to memorable heights, even in the speeches of Joan, who is appropriately its most dynamic character. At its best, the style shows a sure-footed exploitation of conventional resources, as in Suffolk's speeches to and about Margaret. The literary finesse of the author appears far more clearly in his choice of events— even his creation of them—to epitomize phases of the political situation, and the juxtaposition of these events in subtle counterpoint. The best scenes are those that are marked by acute value conflicts—as when Joan meets and repudiates her father, or seeks desperate subterfuges to avoid execution by her English captors (a scene memorable enough to provide a model for Webster's scene of Cariola's death in *The Duchess of Malfi*). The tone of the play does not seem at once to contrast with the patriotic concern of the earlier chronicle plays (one of which may have dealt with Talbot's career); their anti-French, anti-Catholic moralizing reappears in many scenes, and sententious choric speeches still abound. Nevertheless, unlike Hall's *Chronicles* (in which this moralizing, patriotic norm is well revealed) the play often also seems to show less fully defined yet exciting reservations about the simple themes of Protestant nationalism.

The very choice of the weak Henry VI rather than the dashing Talbot as the play's pivot is curious. Despite elements in each vein, this is no simple story of triumphant heroism, like that of Henry V, nor of supposed patriotic issues, like that of King John; it is not a piece of useful political propaganda for the Tudors, like the conventional treatment of Richard III. Henry tries to say all the right things, yet somehow even the best sentiments in the play always have a faint false echo; and the most suspect figures, like the three French women, show hypnotic qualities that are absent from the others. Suffolk anticipates the conventional ecstasies of Romeo, but in infinitely more compromising circumstances, which even call into question any simple uncritical delight in the romanticism of the later play. Such an effect typifies the earlier play's alertness to the potential paradoxes that are inherent in those values which, for the most part, it conscientiously pursues on the surface. It may be that these curious dissonances do reflect merely a patched-up piece of work, designed to act as a sort of prelude to *Part 2*, yet their presence in all the best scenes suggests that the author already has that fascination with reversals and paradoxes that is characteristic of the work of the mature Shakespeare. The dramatic irony of the scene between Talbot and the Countess neatly epitomizes this aspect. Talbot reduces her to bewilderment at the very instant when she is preparing to shackle him, by mocking her desire to imprison a mere shadow. She exclaims:

> This is a riddling merchant for the nonce;
> He will be here, and yet he is not here:
> How can these contraries agree?
> (II.iii.57–9)

Only then does Talbot cut through the ambiguities of meaning to call up his real strength in the form of his concealed army. The realities of power and the contrasting ambiguities of language and appearance are perfectly expressed in this scene.

2

Henry VI

⟋ *Part Two*

THE SOCIETY of the first part of *Henry VI* is on the verge of disintegration, but it is still recognizably an ordered society. The innocence of its ruler still allows power only in France to those deadly forces that are grouped around the French women, and more particularly around Joan of Arc (where they appear to take the form of devils). In the second part of *Henry VI*, these forces have invaded English society, largely through the agency of Margaret. Under her impact, that society begins to disintegrate; a kind of blight spreads from her every contact, fostering such monstrosities as the witchcraft that results from the envy of the termagant Duchess of Gloucester. As the play progresses, there is an almost total disintegration of political and moral order within the state. Few elements of the play are more morbidly hypnotic than the painful erosion of the position and personality of the well-meaning Lord Protector, Humphrey Duke of Gloucester, regent during Henry's minority. One watches with fascination the almost tangible currents of evil thus undercutting the foundations of the state. Indeed, the destruction of the state proves to be a mental process, for one perceives that it is essentially semantic (as George Orwell has observed in his famous essay on politics and the English language). Aided skillfully by the no less ambitious Cardinal Beaufort, Bishop of Winchester, Margaret pursues the attainment of dominion over the king by heightening the latent schism between what is said and what is meant and done, thus destroying the possibility of rational judgment and action.

Again certain scenes epitomize this central concern of the play: the nature and hazards of political and moral judgment. The theme is particularly important to the long, complex scene at the start of Act II. Ironically, it is the doomed Gloucester himself who here shows how to distinguish the true from the false, rather as the equally doomed Talbot had mastered the deceit of the Countess of Auvergne in the previous play. He deftly demonstrates the feigned character of the "miracle" that has deceived king and court, and accomplishes a further "miracle" himself by frightening the supposed cripple out of his invalid chair, thereby revealing the deception to the scandalized king, who exclaims, horrified by the trickery he has now discovered:

O God, seest Thou this, and bearest so long?
(II.i.154)

Nevertheless, the moral of the episode escapes the king: that truth is rarely palatable and almost never in harmony with one's hopes—that it is to be attained only by a relentless investigation which requires rigorous, even brutal methods. Yet if Gloucester, at least, has the wit to perceive the truth on this occasion, his uncertain authority as regent prevents him from exercising his insight effectively in the interests of the state.

The susceptibility of the king to Suffolk's blend of sentimentality and covert ambition is shown by his acceptance of the marriage to Margaret that makes her queen. This has already begun the play on an ominous note of courtly affectation triumphing over political incompetence, which is further stressed when Gloucester discovers that the terms of the marriage contract negotiated by Suffolk have in fact cost England the two major parts of her possessions in France, and thereby the security of all the rest. His stupefaction, distress, and final anger are promptly and willfully misinterpreted by the Cardinal as symptoms of haughty pride and ambition, an accusation that is beautifully capped by the soliloquy of York with which the scene ends—in which York proves to be in fact possessed of the very motives and character of which Gloucester has been falsely accused:

> Anjou and Maine are given to the French;
> Paris is lost; the state of Normandy
> Stands on a tickle point, now they are gone: . . .
> 'Tis thine they give away, and not their own. . . .
> A day will come when York shall claim his own. . . .
> Nor shall proud Lancaster usurp my right,
> Nor hold the sceptre in his childish fist,
> Nor wear the diadem upon his head,
> Whose church-like humours fits not for a crown.
> Then, York, be still awhile, till time do serve.
> (I.i.214–16,221,239,244–8)

Here is another of those ironic juxtapositions that are the hallmark of Shakespearean plot structure, which depends for its impact on the reversal of the expectations of conventional judgment. The man who appears to behave immoderately is in fact virtuous, while the true source of danger lies concealed under the mask of decorum.

These early scenes are written far more coherently and tightly than most of the scenes in the previous play. Thus York's aggressive speech is immediately followed by one in which the Duchess seeks to betray Gloucester into the course of action of which he has been accused, and which York has already adopted. The crude usurpation of her husband's or lover's volition appears here as a symptom of disorder in a woman's mind, particularly if it is associated with the Duchess' misreading of true virility:

> Follow I must; I cannot go before,
> While Gloucester bears this base and humble mind.
> Were I a man, a duke, and next of blood,
> I would remove these tedious stumbling-blocks,

And smooth my way upon their headless necks;
And, being a woman, I will not be slack
To play my part in Fortune's pageant.
(I.ii.61–7)

"Were I a man"—this matches in wish with Joan's actual deeds and Lady Macbeth's prayers to be divested of her sex; in each instance the forces of evil are shown to crystallize in such a context.

The seance that the Duchess attends is no mere flummery: it is as if, when confronted by "a woman of an invincible spirit," metaphysical evil is irresistibly drawn to so useful an agent for its ends—which will inevitably include the ultimate destruction of this agent as well. Indeed, from the moment when the Duchess plans her "part in Fortune's pageant," the audience's responses to the Wheel of Fortune are triggered—the Duchess is in their anticipation doomed to the very fall that she, in her *hubris*, brutally plans for others. We learn this for certain immediately after we hear her resolution to pursue her ambitions, when, in his soliloquy, Hume, her abettor and betrayer, illustrates the extreme character of one of the old morality play's figures, with his monomania for gold:

Dame Eleanor gives gold to bring the witch:
Gold cannot come amiss, were she a devil.
Yet have I gold flies from another coast;
I dare not say, from the rich cardinal
And from the great and new-made Duke of Suffolk,
Yet I do find it so; . . .
Sort how it will, I shall have gold for all.
(I.ii.91–6,107)

The king's religious and amatory sentimentality, and his political weakness seem necessarily to coexist with (if not actually favor) all these other extremes of attitude in his subjects—diabolism, cynicism, and ruthless self-seeking. Henry's high-minded rule is doomed above all by his sentimental association with his beautiful but sinister queen, who for her own selfish reasons insists on cutting across established order. This she does first (through another neat juxtaposition) in the next scene after the Duchess has attacked Gloucester's integrity. The queen begins by angrily asking Suffolk:

> What, shall King Henry be pupil still
> Under the surly Gloucester's governance?
> Am I a queen in title and in style,
> And must be made a subject to a duke?
>   (I.iii.49–52)

The queen's bitterness derives its greatest intensity, however, from the overbearing manner of the Duchess, whose ambition has been displayed in the previous scene; this complex of ambitions and rivalries meshes perfectly as the action evolves. We know that Suffolk is lying in wait for the Duchess; when the court assembles, the humiliations inflicted on her by the queen provide a foretaste not only of the revolution of the Duchess' fortune, but a pattern for the fates of all the ambitious aristocrats who are involved in the plot, including the queen and Suffolk themselves.

York will be the supreme victim; but at this point his fortunes are scarcely in the ascendant, even though Henry's political naivety is already obviously to York's advantage. Henry is frankly indifferent about the appointment to the regency in France:

> For my part, noble lords, I care not which;
> Or Somerset or York, all's one to me.
>   (I.iii.104–5)

This abdication of his authority provokes a violent argument about the regency, which is governed by its bearing on the political ambitions of those involved. York loses this powerful appointment because the queen has already picked up gossip to his disadvantage. York, however, strikes an attitude of wounded innocence (later to be perfected by his second son, who will become Richard III):

I'll tell thee, Suffolk, why I am unmeet:
First, for I cannot flatter thee in pride; . . .
(I.iii.168–9)

The question of York's guilt, of course, eludes the judgment of the king; that matter has to be left, as a result, to the arbitration of Providence in a trial by combat. Yet, once this solution is decided upon, the next scene but one confronts the audience and the king with the feigned miracle, skeptically shown up by Humphrey for the fraud it is. How can single combat be safely left to Providence if blatant fraud and blasphemy thus flourish without divine response? The king is shaken, as we saw, but still continues naively resolute in his belief in absolute values, for the later scene concludes with Henry setting out for London in his usual spirit, on receiving news of the Duchess' diabolism:

To-morrow toward London back again,
To look into this business thoroughly
And call these foul offenders to their answers
And poise the cause in justice' equal scales,
Whose beam stands sure, whose rightful cause prevails.
(II.i.201–5)

Nothing could be further from the truth in terms of the trial's consequences—the public humiliation of his wife unnerves Duke Humphrey, who suffers in proportion as he shares the king's loyalty to truth and honor. Thus the punishment of the Duchess gives impetus to the plots of the various conspirators, who are delighted when the king sees fit to follow Humphrey's pathetic exclamation of acceptance of his wife's banishment:

I cannot justify whom the law condemns.
(II.iii.16)

with the dismissal of Humphrey from his offices as regent. The one man who shares the king's principles is thus dismissed at the very moment when his integrity is most vindicated. Well may Margaret rejoice:

Why, now is Henry king and Margaret queen;
And Humphrey Duke of Gloucester scarce himself,
That bears so shrewd a maim; two pulls at once;
His lady banish'd, and a limb lopped off—
This staff of honour raught.
              (II.iii.39–43)

The king and his court are left to preside over the
grotesque trial of strength between York's drunken ar-
morer and his terrified apprentice. Unpredictably, the
gossip that favored York for the throne is proven to have
been true—but Henry's response is not to follow this
"divine" admonition and scrutinize York more closely.
Instead, he is content to rely even more confidently than
before on the principle that he can for once see manifested
in some practical sense:

God in justice hath reveal'd to us
The truth and innocence of this poor fellow.
              (II.iii.105–6)

Indeed, later in the play, just after the appalling murder
of Gloucester, the king is still undiscriminating enough to
affirm:

What stronger breastplate than a heart untainted!
Thrice is he arm'd that hath his quarrel just,
And he but naked, though lock'd up in steel,
Whose conscience with injustice is corrupted.
              (III.ii.232–5)

The nature of the moral order of the universe in its
relation to political and judicial acts becomes the central
concern of the play through this kind of counterpoint of
fact and interpretation; the scenes of Gloucester's fall
show the secularization of the drama, in that Henry's faith
in the realization of God's justice on earth has been proven
to be shockingly at odds with the truth of particular
situations. The issue is further intensified by the scene of
separation, in which the exiled Duchess grimly warns her
husband that mere innocence will be no security against

his subtle enemies; but with strenuous conviction Humphrey refuses, like the king, to believe in the powers of evil:

> Ah, Nell, forbear! thou aimest all awry;
> I must offend before I be attainted;
> And had I twenty times so many foes,
> And each of them had twenty times their power,
> All these could not procure me any scathe,
> So long as I am loyal, true and crimeless.
>
> (II.iv.58–63)

The two following scenes, which demonstrate the folly both of Gloucester's self-assurance and of the king's faith in the triumph of virtue, are made painful and often intensely dramatic by such skillful alternations as that of the accusations against Gloucester and York's second soliloquy, in which he avows the very treason of which Gloucester is wrongfully accused. Neither Gloucester nor the king can cope with the relentless misrepresentations of the queen, who is aided and abetted by the Cardinal. Where evil is so strenuous, virtue tends to be defensive; or sometimes it becomes guilty of no less stridency, to its own disadvantage.

The murder of Gloucester alone can shock Henry into effective action in banishing the transparently guilty Suffolk. And here begins the countermovement of the play. Gloucester's murder is a pivotal event in the tetralogy, an action so monstrous as to set on foot forces that demonstrate that the characters still exist in an ultimately ordered universe—although one by no means as wholly subject to Providence as Henry imagines, or as the old morality plays had shown. Virtue may be destroyed often in the world of *Henry VI*, but Nemesis always overtakes the guilty. The Duchess of Gloucester's diabolism meets its deserts, as does the comparable guilt of the queen and Suffolk. In fact, the audience cannot but be struck by the duplication of the Gloucesters' scene of separation in the later one at Act III, Scene ii; only now it is Suffolk who is exiled from England and, along with him, his mistress the queen laments their resulting separation.

Even in the midst of Suffolk's romantic exclamations comes a more dreadful, yet equally justified stroke of fate. We have already been told by the second murderer of the full innocence of Gloucester's death: "O that it were to do! What have we done? Didst ever hear a man so penitent?" (III.ii.3–4). Now we hear about the state of the dying Cardinal, who had taken the initiative in proposing that murder. Like Lady Macbeth's, his mind has disintegrated under the stress of his own villainy. Vaux reports

> That Cardinal Beaufort is at point of death;
> For suddenly a grievous sickness took him,
> That makes him gasp and stare and catch the air,
> Blaspheming God and cursing men on earth.
>   (III.ii.369–72)

It is with this sinister association in mind that we hear the characteristic sentimentality of romantic love from Suffolk's lips after the queen has warned him of the approach of the king, with death as the penalty of discovery:

> If I depart from thee I cannot live;
> And in thy sight to die, what were it else
> But like a pleasant slumber in thy lap?
> Here could I breathe my soul into the air . . .
>   (III.ii.388–91)

His farewell is similarly redolent with affectation, yet it is brutally loaded with unconscious prophecy: "This way fall I to death."

It might be thought that, with the hysterical death of the Cardinal, and the calculated humiliation of Suffolk's assassination on the Kentish coast, the action has established the scope of retributive fate. But Shakespeare takes a far more tragic view of the working out of the movements initiated by these victims. Suffolk is, after all, only a type of the anarchistic self-interest and egotistical sentimentality of the English upper classes. The supercilious behavior of Suffolk on the verge of death sets essentially aristocratic viciousness in contrast to lower-class indignation at such traitorous depravity. Suffolk's extravagant words to his assassins again remind us of the allegorical absolutism of characters in the morality plays:

> Obscure and lowly swain, King Henry's blood,
> The honorable blood of Lancaster,
> Must not be shed by such a jaded groom.
> Hast thou not kissed thy hand and held my stirrup? . . .
> It is impossible that I should die
> By such a lowly vassal as thyself.
> (IV.i.50-3,110-11)

Suffolk's rodomontade is answered by the crude realism of his captors:

> Convey him hence and on our longboat's side
> Strike off his head.
> (IV.i.68-9)

His vanity is judged as

> . . . kennel, puddle, sink; whose filth and dirt
> Troubles the silver spring where England drinks.
> (IV.i.71-2)

The revolutionary overtones of this encounter are not incidental; they are part of the vast convulsion set afoot by Henry's innocent incompetence and the aristocracy's resulting egotistical irresponsibility. York has been shipped off to Ireland by the queen and Suffolk, who think to cut him off from political influence, but before he leaves he sets the fuse to a disastrous explosive: the resentment of the lower classes, from which the feudal aristocracy will never recover, either in the tetralogy or in historic fact:

> You put sharp weapons in a madman's hands.
> Whiles I in Ireland nourish a mighty band,
> I will stir up in England some black storm
> Shall blow ten thousand souls to heaven or hell;
> And this fell tempest shall not cease to rage
> Until the golden circuit on my head, . . .
> Do calm the fury of this mad-bred flaw.

And for the minister of my intent,
I have seduced a headstrong Kentishman,
John Cade of Ashford, . . .
This devil here shall be my substitute.
(III.i.347–52,353–6,371)

Again one sees the imagery turning history into allegory
—the "devil" Cade functions as a kind of abstract of the
indignant responses of the lower class (such as we see at
the execution of Suffolk). Though he too is corrupt and
cynical, he has (like Joan) the insight of the politically
gifted—and when he declaims to a horrified aristocrat, "I
am the besom that must sweep the court clean of such
filth as thou art" (IV.vii.32–3), one feels the ring of an
authority like Joan's. The scenes in which Cade and his
sympathizers terrorize the upper classes do have a kind of
macabre humor, but this should not conceal their basically
serious intent. We may laugh when Dick suggests as the
first act of revolution, "Let's kill all the lawyers" (IV.ii.84),
or when Cade declares to Lord Say: "It will be proved to
thy face that thou hast men about thee that usually talk
of a noun and a verb, and such abominable words as no
Christian can endure or hear" (IV.vii.39–42). Again, a
wretched clerk is hung for confessing he can sign his
name, just as the Roman mob in *Julius Caesar* murders
Cinna the poet "for his bad verses" (III.iii.33). But what
is involved here is no mere vulgar hatred of learning; it
is rather the commonsense suspicion of courtly and academic affectation, of the kind favored by Suffolk and the
king, which has already reduced the country to its present
state of anarchy.

As we have seen, the plot illustrates the political validity
of this popular view. It is a theme to which Shakespeare
will often return. In *Love's Labour's Lost*, for example (a
play apparently spun out of Shakespeare's own consciousness, since no source for it is known), the essence of the
action is a recognition of the dangers inherent in that
verbal facility that was so characteristic of Shakespeare
himself, from his earliest compositions to those of his ma-

turity. Yet the point of the failures of the young nobles' love affairs in *Love's Labour's Lost* is precisely to show that verbal virtuosity is worse than useless at moments of crisis. It proves a positive barrier to the sincere consolation of one of the ladies who has lost her father; and the failure of the gallants' wit to win love by words is further highlighted by the penalties imposed by the ladies on their suitors, who must serve the poor and afflicted, live in touch with the humble realities of life, and forgo both academic idealism and courtly affectation. Biron, the most subtle and fluent of the young men, comes to recognize the power of "honest plain words" and the need to avoid their opposite.

It is clear that Suffolk and King Henry VI are two of these affected aristocrats, whose gallantry and academicism have strayed from the world of comedy into that of political history, with tragic results. Just as in *Love's Labour's Lost* the lower classes are finally driven to harsh and authoritative denunciation of their superiors: "This is not generous, not gentle, not humble" (V.ii.632), so figures like the sea captain or Cade carry conviction in their pitiless pursuit of the intelligentsia and the aristocracy, whose wits have been devoted to the corruption and betrayal of their country. The point is perceptive, and the play functions on a moral level superior to that of the old political morality plays and patriotic histories, which scarcely reflected any such refinement of values and division of sympathies.

The precarious balance of values and sympathies that emerges in these last scenes illustrates Shakespeare's characteristic strength as moralist, dramatist, and political historian. To see the Joan of *Part 1* as merely a monstrous caricature of a noble young woman is not to do justice to the strength and political finesse of her portrait. Similarly, Cade in *Part 2* is a curious mixture of viciousness and insight, which marks out this character as superior to most of the others in the play. Although he appears in York's soliloquy as a monster, he is moved by Lord Say's desperate plea of innocence. There is a fascinating ambivalence in his response:

> I feel remorse in myself with his words; but I'll bridle it: he shall die, an it be for pleading so well for his life. Away with him! he has a familiar under his tongue; he speaks not o' God's name. Go, take him away, I say, and strike off his head presently.
>
> (IV.vii.111–15)

One must admire, if not the historical probability of the character, at least the virtuosity of mind of its creator, who will devote this kind of finesse to the development of another, far more interesting character, who appears a few scenes later—the younger son of York, who is finally to become Richard III. Like Richard, Cade is under no illusions about his followers: "Was ever feather so lightly blown to and fro as this multitude?" (IV.viii.57–8), and when they betray him, he cuts his way through them like chaff. However, Shakespeare's sense of irony metes out justice on Cade himself, who accurately anticipates his own fall in this ominous self-analysis:

> Fie on ambition! fie on myself, that have a sword, and yet am ready to famish! These five days I have hid me in these woods and durst not peep out, for all the country is laid for me.
>
> (IV.x.1–4)

Yet Cade is too symbolic of lower class resentment and primitive vitality to meet his death at the hands of the effete aristocracy. There is a profound symbolism in his destruction at the hands of Iden, the rural squire who delights in his avoidance of the corruptions of the court, and the fickleness of fortune:

> Lord, who would live turmoiled in the court,
> And may enjoy such quiet walks as these?
> This small inheritance my father left me
> Contenteth me, and worth a monarchy.

I seek not to wax great by others' waning,
Or gather wealth, I care not, with what envy:
Sufficeth that I have maintains my state
And sends the poor well pleased from my gate.

(IV.x.18–25)

Here is a man who has escaped the Wheel of Fortune, and
he alone can justly hope to confront and destroy Cade, the
other pole of those resentments that Iden's more rational
and temperate outlook has already addressed against the
aristocracy. Ironically, he would neither have betrayed
Cade nòr grudged him, starving, his thefts from the garden. While Iden at first refuses to use his men against
Cade, he perceives the pathological violence of Cade's
speech and acts unflinchingly:

Nay, it shall ne'er be said, while England stands
That Alexander Iden, an esquire of Kent,
Took odds to combat a poor famish'd man.
Oppose thy steadfast-gazing eyes to mine,
See if thou canst outface me with thy looks:
Set limb to limb, and thou art far the lesser;
Thy hand is but a finger to my fist,
Thy leg a stick compared with this truncheon;
My foot shall fight with all the strength thou hast;
And if mine arm be heaved in the air,
Thy grave is digg'd already in the earth.
As for words, whose greatness answers words,
Let this my sword report what speech forbears.

(IV.x.45–57)

This is a magnificent figure, and Cade, however ironically,
is made to salute "the most complete champion that ever
I heard." The contrast between Iden's compassionate yet
potent personality and the unbalanced sentimentality or
egotism of most of the other characters in the play strikes
a powerful positive note that underscores the remainder
of the action as a series of monstrous discords. While
Shakespeare's sympathetic feelings for a sturdy country
gentleman are unmistakable here, the episode accurately

reflects the increasingly significant status of the squire-
archy in English history.

The next scene shows York drunk with ambition for
power, a portrait deftly transposed by Shakespeare from
the no less historical character of Tamburlaine, whose
own exploits were dignified by Marlowe's "mighty line."
Tamburlaine is preoccupied with "the sweet fruition of an
earthly crown," and Shakespeare invests York with the
same extravagant ambition:

> From Ireland thus comes York to claim his right,
> And pluck the crown from feeble Henry's head:
> Ring, bells, aloud; burn, bonfires, clear and bright,
> To entertain great England's lawful king.
> Ah! *sancta majestas*, who would not buy thee dear?
> Let them obey that know not how to rule.
> (V.i.1–6)

The fact that this scene follows at once after Iden's destruction of Cade establishes the analogy between York
and his agent. York hopes to dominate an English race
that, in Iden's case at least, *does* know how to rule, and
is thus the less inclined to servile surrender to usurping
tyrants. He also unconsciously prophecies how "dear" he
is soon to buy his pursuit of "*sancta majestas*," not even
in destroying but in merely defeating King Henry. York's
increasing unbalance appears in the furies to which he is
now subject:

> Scarce can I speak, my choler is so great:
> O, I could hew up rocks and fight with flint,
> I am so angry at these abject terms;
> And now, like Ajax Telamonius,
> On sheep or oxen could I spend my fury. . . .
> (V.i.23–7)

Yet if Iden's poise and effectiveness contrast with York's
unbalance, York's demoniacal energy is a sharp foil to
Henry's feeble good intentions. York's denunciation of
Henry on returning from Ireland is ruthless and decisive:

King did I call thee? no, thou art not king,
Not fit to govern and rule multitudes,
Which darest not, no, nor canst not rule a traitor.
That head of thine doth not become a crown;
Thy hand is made to grasp a palmer's staff . . .
Here is a hand to hold a sceptre up
And with the same to act controlling laws.
                    (V.i.93–7,102–3)

Henry's response when the queen and others allow him an opportunity to speak, more than justifies this denunciation by its very feebleness:

O, where is faith? O, where is loyalty?
                    (V.i.166)

Out of this illustration of the inability to "rule a traitor," the final collapse of the English state is born; civil war breaks out and all the emotions that have smoldered in concealment burst into open flame. Enemies become consciously pitiless. Young Clifford, on seeing his dead father, takes up the inhuman, murderous note of academic Senecan tragedy:

Henceforth I will not have to do with pity:
Meet I an infant of the house of York,
Into as many gobbets will I cut it
As wild Medea young Absyrtus did:
In cruelty will I seek out my fame.
                    (V.ii.56–60)

In the Biblical phrase, "The fathers have eaten sour grapes and the children's teeth are set on edge." Just as Lear has daughters who share his own intransigence, so the last scene of *Henry VI, Part 2* introduces us to the epitome of York's own vices, Richard, whose savagery matches that of his enemy, Young Clifford:

Sword, hold thy temper; heart, be wrathful still:
Priests pray for enemies, but princes kill.
                    (V.ii.70–1)

The pronouncement echoes York, but Richard is to become an even more sinister, God–sent scourge for the vices of England than Cade had been. And as the play concludes Henry begins to see what horrors he has loosed on his kingdom, and to understand that the practical political issues that produced his defeat now add up to a larger, metaphysical meaning (which will find its absolute form in the shape of the last play of the series, *Richard III*). Margaret urges flight and regrouping, but Henry, passive as always, wonders, wisely for once, "Can we outrun the heavens?"

3

Henry VI

Part Three

THE TWO earlier parts of *Henry VI* make serious claims upon our critical attention, despite their failure to conform to some aesthetic norms through their diffusion of interest over a wide variety of actions and personalities. They are not lacking in deliberate progressions, whose political and moral implications are subtle and dexterously evoked. The counterpoint of personality and issue is complex and epic in its range; it creates a sense of an actual rather than a theoretical study of a social organism, in which English history in all its vivid variety is unfolded to the audience. The success of the plays in both Elizabethan and modern times shows that an audience as attuned to political debate and sociological tensions as Shakespeare's audience has been in both ages cannot but be fascinated by the diversity of incident and the deftness of juxtaposition. In their vividness and variety, as well as in their purpose, these two history plays mark a distinctive achievement in the long evolution of the form from the morality plays through the chronicles to the more truly literate Elizabethan theater.

Yet, if the plays have many excellences, they also have some conspicuous defects. There are frequent lapses of taste, of the kind to which popular art is prone—such as the crude caricatures of the French that diminish the power of the first part. More serious, from the point of view of drama, is the proliferation of overlong, pedantically sententious speeches, in which historical trivia and platitude deaden interest. Sometimes, too, the academic conventions of Latin drama along Senecan lines overload exchanges of even the most bitter enemies with clumsy formality and rhetorical cadences.

The third part of *Henry VI* is heavily burdened with all these limitations, so that it seems a more immature work than the preceding plays in the series. If anything, its defects predominate, as if the author, in trying to write more seriously and solemnly, had failed to sustain the coarser energies and sharp contrasts of the other plays. The long, flat, fatuous speech of Henry on the battlefield is indefensible in many respects, and the crude parallelisms of this speech are matched by the symmetrically conceived situations (a son who has killed his father, and a father who has killed his son) that are presented immediately afterwards. In general, Henry's part now shows the defects of his character, without any compensating artistic excellence in the execution of this portrait. While some episodes, such as his quite artificial forecast of the great future of Henry Tudor, are somewhat implausibly handled, his death at the hand of Richard of Gloucester suggests that Richard is almost justified in getting rid of such a bore. Indeed, his son had earlier been avowedly murdered for tactlessly irritating Richard and the other victorious Yorkists.

However, if the part of Henry must put great strain on any director's ingenuity, the part of Richard is a considerable compensation. While Henry's sententiousness is stilted, Richard's extraordinary "aria" at the end of Act III, Scene ii represents a real artistic breakthrough in the series (suggesting perhaps the mature revision of a text that had preceded the first two parts in date of composition). This virtuoso soliloquy is derived from Marlowe, and it clearly shares the literary verve that he demonstrated in plays like *Tamburlaine*—although, in the solilo-

quies of Richard's father York, the plays had already ex-
perimented successfully with the vivid, subjective revelation that the formula permitted. There is indeed much of
medieval absolutism in the brutally frank confessions of
York and Richard; they remind us of such pitiless figures
as Chaucer's Pardoner, or of the unequivocal Vices of the
morality plays. But they differ from the latter, at least, in
an emotional intensity and vividness of characterization
that is closely related to the literary mastery of language
and the intellectual originality with which their speeches
are invested.

Richard's sixty lines of exquisitely phrased self-analysis
ends in a Senecan coda, whose savagery has become almost
as familiar as Hotspur's famous declamation about honor,
and offers any reasonably adequate actor the opportunity
to electrify the most indifferent audience. That Shakespeare was aware of this achievement is apparent in his
use of a parallel speech to open *Richard III*, and in the
recurrence of such soliloquies by later characters, such as
Iago and Edmund.

The strength of all these characters lies in their absolute
self-knowledge, which gives them the advantage over those
around them, and an authoritative insight and intelligence
that irresistibly wins the audience's sympathy by providing
both choric truth and the witty contempt for affectation
that both Joan and Cade have already displayed on occasion. Richard has the added resource of irony—a refinement almost unknown to the earlier history plays. After
his brother Edward IV's foolish marriage with Lady Grey,
Richard answers his brother's plea for approval with canting compliment that scarcely masks his contempt for the
new queen and her uxorious husband:

No, God forbid that I should wish them sever'd
Whom God hath join'd together; ay, and 'twere a pity
To sunder them that yoke so well together.

(IV.i.21-3)

Richard shows an absoluteness in his attitudes that his
more worldly brother rarely shares, and one soon recog-

nizes the transmutation of Richard's historical character
from that of a merely vivid personality to one that illustrates the sinister means and ruthless aims of the whole
Yorkist faction, and of most of the English aristocracy.
Again and again it is Richard who epitomizes relentless
ambition, both in his own person and in his advice to
others. "Fearless minds climb soonest unto crowns"
(IV.vii.62), he tells his brother. More crucially, it is he
who takes the initiative in encouraging his father, the
Duke of York, to break his oath to serve King Henry.
The oath had been given when that increasingly greedy
monarch was buying off the monarchy from the Yorkists
during his lifetime, at the expense of his own son's claim
to succeed him. Richard's plausible and enthusiastic advocacy of a new rebellion is infinitely subtler as a rationalization for ambition than anything in the preceding
plays:

> An oath is of no more moment, being not took
> Before a true and lawful magistrate
> That hath authority over him that swears:
> Henry had none, but did usurp the place;
> Then seeing 'twas he that made you to depose,
> Your oath, my lord, is vain and frivolous.
> Therefore, to arms! And father, do but think
> How sweet a thing it is to wear a crown;
> Within whose circuit is Elysium
> And all that poets feign of bliss and joy.
>
> (I.ii.22–31)

The echo of Marlowe's Tamburlaine is unmistakable,
but the dramatic tension of moral and legalistic values is
more characteristic of Shakespeare—and Richard, York's
evil genius, subtly voices York's own desires. Even after
his father's death, Richard's scorching nature burns
fiercely:

> I cannot weep; for all my body's moisture
> Scarce serves to quench my furnace-burning heart:
> Nor can my tongue unload my heart's great burthen;
> For selfsame wind that I should speak withal

Is kindling coals that fires all my breast,
And burns me up with flames that tears would quench.

(II.i.79–84)

Richard has become almost the essence of fiery energy; after he has inflamed his father's ambition, and then swept his brother to the throne, it is only the folly of the latter that finally convinces Richard of the need to bank his fiery energies in the interest of his own succession to power.

Throughout *Part 3*, Richard usurps that pivotal, initiatory role that had been played by the women of the earlier plays—Joan, Eleanor and Margaret. England's corruption is no longer the product of a facile and deceptive rhetoric, but of a relentless, utterly amoral lust for power. This savage outlook has no room for anything but the shadow of Joan's nationalism, Henry's idealism, or Suffolk's sentimental passion; it regularly achieves monstrosities of the order of the casual assassinations of the innocent Henry and his young son. These acts are so brutal and callous as to transform even Queen Margaret from a viciously ambitious woman into something like that quintessence of outraged motherhood and wifehood that Aeschylus makes of his Furies in the Agamemnon trilogy. Yet, appropriately, it is she who first lends an edge to Richard's savagery, providing it with a model by her merciless treatment of the captured Duke of York before his death. This scene is one of the most gruesome in Shakespeare, and clearly aims at Senecan horror, with such details as the offer of a napkin to York steeped in his own son's blood. Yet the scene has resonances of a curious and memorable kind.

It has been commonly observed that the Duke is forced to undergo sufferings comparable to Christ's; Northumberland even observes:

Beshrew me, but his passion moves me so
That hardly can I check my eyes from tears.

(I.iv.150–1)

And if the blood-soaked cloth is grotesquely analogous to
the one offered by St. Veronica to Christ, Richard also
has his mock crown, from the hands of Margaret:

> Thou wouldst be fee'd, I see, to make me sport:
> York cannot speak, unless he wear a crown.
> A crown for York! and, lords, bow low to him:
> Hold you his hands, whilst I do set it on.
>   [*Putting a paper crown on his head.*]
> Ay, marry, sir, now looks he like a king!
> Ay, this is he that took King Henry's chair,
> And this is he was his adopted heir.
>   (I.iv.92–8)

Yet many commentators fail to see that all these analogies
to Christ's passion are savagely ironic—the scene is in fact
as double-edged as Shakespeare's greatest (for example, the
banishment of Falstaff). Far from being an innocently
suffering Christ, York is a brutally ambitious man who is
now meeting his just deserts for having broken his oath to
King Henry.

York may finally die religiously:

> Open Thy gate of mercy, gracious God!
> My soul flies through these wounds to seek out Thee.
>   (I.iv.177–8)

but his life has been evil in the highest degree, and every
clashing analogy to the death of Christ drives home that
fact. Margaret is consciously the agent of just retribution
visited upon a man who has broken a twice-taken oath—
although Shakespeare refuses, appropriately, to allow Margaret unequivocal authority in the role of agent of retribution. For the fact is that she proves even more callous and
brutal than York at this point, so that he in turn, at the
moment of merited destruction, achieves a moral advantage over her, who will shortly suffer as exquisitely as he:

> How could thou drain the life-blood of the child,
> To bid the father wipe his eyes withal,
> And yet be seen to bear a woman's face?

Women are soft, mild, pitiful and flexible;
Thou stern, obdurate, flinty, rough, remorseless.

(I.iv.138–42)

Margaret's loss of both son and husband will alone suffice
to return her to a feminine role in the last play of the
tetralogy. Only there does she achieve a truly monumental
status, through suffering.

It becomes necessary to examine the series of plays as
a unit, in order to perceive the underlying logic of such
progressions. Superficially, the detailed action of each play
often appears confused and ambiguous, yet increasingly
one notes the persistence of certain medieval themes and
rhythms as the series progresses. Most powerful and most
traditional is the theme of the inevitable downfall of human hopes, which receives climactic statement from the
lips of the dying Warwick:

My blood, my want of strength, my sick heart shows,
That I must yield my body to the earth
And, by my fall, the conquest to my foe.
Thus yields the cedar to the axe's edge,
Whose arms gave shelter to the princely eagle,
Under whose shade the ramping lion slept,
Whose top-branch overpeer'd Jove's spreading tree
And kept low shrubs from winter's powerful wind. . . .
Lo, now my glory smeared in dust and blood!
My parks, my walks, my manors that I had,
Even now forsake me, and of all my lands
Is nothing left me but my body's length.
Why, what is pomp, rule, reign, but earth and dust?
And, live we how we can, yet die we must.

(V.ii.8–15,23–8)

This firm and sonorous statement of one of the great
commonplaces of both the Middle Ages and the Renaissance reminds us that the series opens with the death of
Henry V, which is then followed by the deaths of such
other imposing figures as Talbot, Joan, Gloucester, Cade,
and York. Death comes in a variety of frightful forms to
these and to many lesser characters in the series—and it

rarely comes fortuitously. There is even a certain logic involved in some of the disasters—a neglect of proper caution in Gloucester, an oathbreaking rebellion in York. As Henry's position weakens, he, no less than the wicked men around him, finds himself entrapped by the correlation between his conduct and his fate. When Henry surrenders to his wife's indignation and reclaims for his own son the succession he had surrendered to the Yorkists, he loses what self-confidence has remained to him. Far from being reassured when Margaret shows him York's head, this affects him

> . . . as the rocks cheer them that fear their wreck:
> To see this sight, it irks my very soul.
> Withhold revenge, dear God! 'tis not my fault,
> Nor wittingly have I infringed my vow.
> (II.ii.5–8)

More profoundly still, Henry's lack of toughness lays open to question the whole nature of his title to the crown, which is founded on the shaky ground of the usurpation of the throne of Richard II by the Lancastrians, a junior branch of the Plantagenet family. The uneasiness of his title appears significant only when the Lancastrians' grip on affairs begins to slacken; in many ways, the subtlest issue in the third part of the series is the nature of rightful title and the sanctions that vindicate authority. It is here that the beginnings of a striking principle in Shakespeare's historiography are sketched out.

Appropriately enough, the first scene establishes a confrontation of claims between Henry and the Yorkists. Title and power confront each other: Henry is titular king but, as Warwick reminds the Lancastrians:

> You forget
> That we are those which chased you from the field.
> (I.i.89–90)

It would appear that the result is a stalemate. Certainly Henry feels it to be so:

I know not what to say; my title's weak.
(I.i.134)

Yet Henry's plausible evaluation of the situation is rejected both by his supporters and, more seriously, by the course into which Providence directs events. Clifford bitterly reminds Henry of the glory of his father's reign, despite the fact that his title showed a similar weakness. Of York he says:

Patience is for poltroons, such as he:
He durst not sit there had your father lived.
My gracious lord, here in the parliament
Let us assail the family of York.
(I.i.62–5)

The course of action proposed is crude and murderous, but Henry is not so much shocked as merely too frightened to give the order because of Yorkist strength in the city. It is very interesting to note that it is Exeter, who has hitherto acted as a kind of impartial chorus, that urges Henry to act. He says of the Yorkist troops: "When the duke is slain, they'll quickly fly" (I.i.69). The play is here making a very harsh political point: the good king is not necessarily an obviously good man.

However, we must also note that Clifford, embittered by his own father's death, is a dangerous counselor, and Providence soon pronounces judgment on him in the prophetic voice of the youthful Rutland, whom he murders in cold blood. As he dies, Rutland pronounces a ritual curse which, for greater weight, is declaimed in Latin:

Di faciant laudis summa sit ista tuae.   (I.iii.48)
[The gods grant that this may be the height of your glory.]

Clifford stifles his pity for this "poor boy" (I.iii.21), because of his pathological hatred of the family that killed his father; yet, when Clifford says "I live in hell" (I.iii.33), one feels the force of self-judgment. When he dies, one again recognizes the symmetry of fate and temperament in the echoes of the earlier scenes:

> Bootless are plaints, and cureless are my wounds;
> No way to fly, nor strength to hold out flight:
> The foe is merciless, and will not pity;
> For at their hands I have deserved no pity.
> (II.vi.23–6)

This coordination of life and death is in startling contrast to the superficially anarchic texture of the plays, and suggests that the author is far more in command than the characters' own sense of their freedom to act might suggest.

Yet, if Clifford meets his just deserts, his comments on Henry also carry complete authority. His dying pronouncement on Henry's failure as a king has choric status:

> And, Henry, hadst thou sway'd as kings should do,
> Or as thy father and his father did,
> Giving no ground unto the house of York,
> They never then had sprung like summer flies;
> I and ten thousand in this luckless realm
> Had left no mourning widows for our death;
> And thou this day hadst kept thy chair in peace.
> (II.vi.14–20)

Henry's refusal to dislodge York from the king's throne in parliament was avowedly not based on moral scruples, but on a failure of nerve. Henry's inability to act constituted a betrayal of trust: the king's obligation is to keep the king's peace. York had challenged that and Henry was guilty, in failing to meet this challenge, of all the disasters that it entailed. That firmness would have been sufficient is made clear by the defeat and death of York, once the queen takes resolute action.

Providence sides with those who assert their authority effectively, whatever their title; this was the case with Henry IV and Henry V. Authority appears to be largely a state of mind, if one lying outside Henry's comprehension and, ironically, also outside that of the heir to

York's claim on the throne, his son Edward. The center of the third play of the series is somewhat grotesque, in that it brings two kings face to face, both of whom lack the essential attribute of a king: the will to rule; yet this faculty was possessed to a high degree by both the queen and York, not to mention Richard. There is a further quality that Henry and Edward share: neither attains power entirely on his own initiative; instead, both inherit their status from a dynamic father, and appear to accept it as their due, without recognizing the effort it demands for continuance. Edward is as casual with regard to his state and acts as whimsically as Henry does—committing above all the identical fault of making a foolish marriage that infuriates the French, as well as his own best supporters. The analogy here is too striking for us not to perceive another pattern emerging in the sequence.

By the middle of the play, Henry is forced to a very stringent self-evaluation which is in some ways among the more interesting political scenes in the play. The defeated Henry, in disguise, encounters two huntsmen, and his recognition of his folly in returning to his erstwhile kingdom, where a new king now reigns, is established by his soliloquy:

> From Scotland am I stol'n, even of pure love,
> To greet mine own land with my wishful sight.
> No, Harry, Harry, 'tis no land of thine;
> Thy place is fill'd, thy sceptre rung from thee,
> Thy balm wash'd off wherewith thou wast anointed:
> No bending knee will call thee Caesar now,
> No humble suitors press to speak for right,
> No, not a man comes for redress of thee;
> For how can I help them, and not myself?
>
> (III.i.13–21)

In matters of political authority, this speech establishes a principle that is elaborated in greater detail in Hobbes' *Leviathan*—one that still governs the British foreign policy of normally recognizing the effective power of a *de facto* government, whatever the legal title of a powerless *de jure* claimant.

It is true that Henry's title was doubtful, but as long as he effectively exercised power in England he was rightfully king, and York therefore a traitor. Now that Edward has effective power, Henry has no claim to allegiance. This truth is bluntly demonstrated by the huntsmen's arrest of Henry while denying that this act involves any betrayal of their oaths to accept legal authority—oaths that were originally made to Henry: "For we were subjects but while you were king" (III.i.81), now "We are true subjects to the king, King Edward" (III.i.94). Bitterly, Henry's reply points to the arbitrariness of the principle's operation:

> So would you be again to Henry,
> If he were seated as King Edward is.
> (III.i.95–6)

Yet the huntsmen's argument must not be dismissed, as Henry first seeks to do, as a mere rationalization of human fickleness:

> Ah, simple men, you know not what you swear!
> Look, as I blow this feather from my face,
> And as the air blows it to me again,
> Obeying with my wind when I do blow,
> And yielding to another when it blows,
> Commanded always by the greater gust;
> Such is the lightness of you common men.
> (III.i.83–9)

It is not without moral point that, when his working-class allies abandoned him, Jack Cade took the same view (even employing the same image): "Was ever feather so lightly blown to and fro as this multitude? The name of Henry V hales them" (*2HVI*, IV.viii.56–8). The occasion of Cade's loss of support is significant—confronted by firm, traditional authority, the mob's rebelliousness is immediately checked. Henry's delegated authority is more potent in firm hands than his mere presence; as Clifford later says, "The queen hath best success when you are absent" (II.ii.74). A little later, however, we see that in practice even this effective delegation carries its own penalties, for when Henry at one point plaintively insists, "I am a king, and privileged to speak" (II.ii.120), Clifford curtly tells him to "be still."

The struggle between the Lancastrians and the Yorkists is thus precariously balanced, and governed by delicate political issues—even if there is an overriding sense of Providence. York breaks his oath of loyalty and flagrantly affronts established authority by sitting on the throne—and meets the doom that so headstrong and illegal an act deserves. But Henry loses control of his own authority to such dangerously unbalanced subordinates as Clifford and the queen. The throne thus becomes effectively vacant, and since Edward is not formally tainted in the same way as his father York—having merely inherited the struggle with the Lancastrians—the confrontation is absolutely equal, as Henry mournfully judges in his elaborate soliloquy on the battlefield:

> Now one the better, then another best;
> Both tugging to be victors, breast to breast,
> Yet neither conqueror nor conquered:
> So is the equal poise of this fell war.
> Here, on this molehill will I sit me down.
> To whom God will, there be the victory.
> For Margaret my queen, and Clifford too,
> Have chid me from the battle; swearing both
> They prosper best of all when I am thence.
> Would I were dead! if God's good will were so.
>
> (II.v.10–19)

Henry, whatever his title, neither wants to win, nor has he the necessary energies to use his position, even if victory is secured, and this indifference is ultimately decisive.

Authority necessarily passes, if with only the slightest of advantages, to Edward. And the play unequivocally asserts the moral and political authority of this fractional victory, not only in the scene with the huntsmen, where

Henry's lack of effective power in England is made manifest, but also in the investigation of Queen Margaret's claims for assistance from the French King Lewis XI. The authority of a king's judgment on his peer gives validity to Lewis' view of the situation, backed as it is by obvious sympathy for his fellow-countrywoman:

> But if your title to the crown be weak,
> As may appear by Edward's good success,
> Then 'tis but reason that I be released
> From giving aid which late I promised.
>   (III.iii.145–8)

We may feel that the principle invoked—legal title is vindicated by success—is a shallow one, but few better can be found. The trial by combat in *Part 2 was* validated by its outcome, and the ancient Chinese idea of accepting established authority as "the mandate of heaven" is also closely analogous, as we can see in Lewis' conviction that his oath to support Henry is no longer binding when Providence has established another king firmly on the English throne.

The crown of England is not regulated by the same principles as private property; he who wears it fearlessly and without challenge *is* king. The crucial principle of English monarchy—the distinction between the crown as the effective government of England, and the wearer of it as an individual—is strongly present in these plays. Henry acting as king and Henry dispossessed are quite distinct entities. As this principle comes to be understood, the English crown increasingly comes to stand for the government that is vested in the monarch's advisers; ultimately authority comes to reside only in the democratically elected government, even when that is opposed by the monarch himself. This explains how Prince Hal could be imprisoned while heir to the throne, by a judge who represented the crown; it also explains why the English succession appears to be increasingly indifferent to the physical person who occupies the nominal position of ruler; finally, it demonstrates how Charles I could be accused, tried, and executed by his own laws (at least according to the views of the Parliamentarians).

However, Shakespeare shows his characteristic brilliant control of ironic reversals and ambivalences, by making Lewis decide to support Henry almost on the heels of his showing why he should not. The blundering incompetence displayed by Edward in his marriage to Lady Grey, at the very moment when Warwick is arranging a match for him with the French king's daughter, seems to open the way for a whole new conflict. Warwick changes sides too, and so does Edward's own brother Clarence. Events seem to show that Edward's fate will be like Henry's. Warwick captures him by stealth and accuses him forcibly of incompetence:

> Alas! how should you govern any kingdom,
> That know not how to use ambassadors,
> Nor how to be contented with one wife,
> Nor how to use your brothers brotherly,
> Nor how to study for the people's welfare,
> Nor how to shroud yourself from enemies?
> (IV.iii.35–40)

Edward's response seems to be identical to Henry's stoicism in like misfortune:

> What fates impose, that men must needs abide;
> It boots not to resist both wind and tide.
> (IV.iii.58–9)

Yet the situations of the rival kings are quite different. Henry is defeated not only militarily but spiritually; he is a private person, as has been potently demonstrated by representatives of the common people. They do not hesitate to hand him over to the Yorkists who still hold him prisoner. Edward is the effective ruler of England, and he is captured temporarily by subterfuge alone. One remembers how doubtful a resource this was held to be for the French military success against Talbot in *Part 1*. Similarly,

Edward's will to resist is not broken, and he is soon freed by means comparable to those by which he was captured, through the cunning and energy of his brother Richard. He is thus at liberty, as Henry, when he was deposed, was not; and more crucially, Edward returns almost instantly to England—from the point of view of the play—only a hundred lines after his escape to Flanders.

Edward is thus as effective a contender for the throne as he ever was, while in the intervening scene Henry is shown to be as weak as ever. Warwick says to Clarence:

> We'll yoke together, like a double shadow
> To Henry's body, and supply his place:
> I mean, in bearing weight of government,
> While he enjoys the honour and his ease.
> (IV.vi.49–52)

One may compare the situation with that at the start of *King Lear*, when Lear himself makes a similar arrangement:

>   Only we still retain
> The name, and all the additions of a king;
> The sway, revenue, execution of the rest,
> Beloved sons, be yours.
> (I.i.137–40)

Lear's lack of control and love of status produces the same chaos, self-seeking, and anarchy that does Henry's. One notes that Shakespeare feels strongly enough about England's territorial integrity to change the Lear story, so that when Lear is to be restored by French arms (like Henry) —even though they are led by Cordelia—the invaders are defeated, not victorious, as the old versions have it. Edward is not a very good king or strategist, but he wants to be king and shows some toughness in his capture of the city of York. Henry, by contrast, counts merely on his personal virtues, after the chorus-like Exeter has warned him of his troops' doubtful allegiance:

> My mildness hath allayed their swelling griefs,
> My mercy dried their water-flowing tears;

I have not been desirous of their wealth,
Nor much oppress'd them with great subsidies,
Nor forward of revenge, though they much err'd:
Then why should they love Edward more than me?
(IV.viii.41–7)

One sympathizes with Henry's good nature, but the play's drily realistic comment on the speech's idealism is to make this the moment of Edward's recapture and re-incarceration of Henry. Authority counts for more than good intentions and again the balance swings, no matter with what little initial momentum, decisively to Edward. Henry's support is based at best on his termagant queen, the willful pride of Warwick, and the brotherly pique of Yorkist Clarence. This last collapses first:

Why, trow'st thou, Warwick,
That Clarence is so harsh, so blunt, unnatural,
To bend the fatal instruments of war
Against his brother and his lawful king?
Perhaps thou wilt object my holy oath:
To keep that oath were more impiety
Than Jephthah's when he sacrificed his daughter.
(V.i.85–91)

One may note in passing what a dreadful moral tangle Clarence's fickleness has got him into, although in due course he will expiate his blunders. Meanwhile, Fate exacts a prompter end for Warwick, whose magnificent death speech has been noted as a final commentary on his sense of his own importance that, in a moment of personal indignation, had swung him, along with Clarence, against Edward. Alone, the queen and her young son are easily overpowered. In the malicious killing of her son before her, the queen suffers retribution for her gloating insistence to York on his youngest son's death. Gloucester wants to kill the queen, prophetically asking:

Why should she live, to fill the world with words?
(V.v.45)

But his brothers want to keep her alive, sadism appearing in Clarence's refusal of her invitation to kill her:

By heaven, I will not do thee so much ease.
                    (V.v.72)

The Yorkists thus triumph, but their triumph has been achieved in a spirit of harshness that taints it. Edward presides over a dubious reunion when he asks:

Clarence and Gloucester, love my lovely queen;
And kiss your princely nephew, brothers both.
                    (V.vii.26–7)

For the moral cost of victory has already appeared powerfully in Richard's soliloquy at the end of the previous scene, in which he murdered Henry:

Then, since the heavens have shaped my body so,
Let hell make crook'd my mind to answer it.
I have no brother, I am like no brother;
And this word "love," which greybeards call divine,
Be resident in men like one another
And not in me: I am myself alone.
                    (V.vi.78–83)

The cold temper of mind that can murder Henry and thus secure the succession is not likely to rally to simple family loyalties, as Clarence does. Yet, with the end of *Henry VI, Part 3*, the Yorkists are securely rulers of England and the complex political and moral conflicts that have brought them there must not be looked on as the mere accidents of chronicle history. As these episodes appear in the plays, they have been selected from the vast range of historical incidents and personal confrontations, partly in the interest of picturesque scenes, it is true, but also, and more profoundly, by an instinct for the movement of English political tradition from the time of the Norman conquest on. This political instinct is perhaps the subtlest English intellectual resource. It is unquestionably this sense of the complex origins of political authority and the bewildering interplay they produce in any given situation that is the source of any major intellectual and artistic interest that the third part of *Henry VI* may possess—and of much of the excellence of the two earlier plays. The subtle shiftings of advantage and authority, and the ironic sequence of events which attracts the reader, derive from political insight of a kind without contemporary rival. Discovery, here, is art.

4

🎗 *Richard III*

IF SHAKESPEARE's name were associated only with the three parts of *Henry VI*, he could not readily be distinguished from his fellow-dramatists. The plays are unequal in style and execution, even though we may already perceive in them characteristic flashes of Shakespeare's mature genius and basic concerns. It may be said that they mark a natural early climax in the still evolving genre of the history play, and that Shakespeare's three plays lead no less naturally to Marlowe's somewhat superior but analogous *Edward II*. When we turn to *Richard III*, however, we are confronted by a work that, while it is still dependent in detail on the traditional forms, involves a resynthesis of the raw material in so powerful and brilliant a way as to earn it the title of masterpiece. *Henry VI* may be successfully defended against the criticism of incoherence, but *Richard III*, although it is a sequel, needs no such defense. It functions smoothly in terms of modern aesthetics and current preoccupations—at the same time that it deftly draws on the characteristic resources of the English traditional theater—and also exploits the latest in Elizabethan intellectual fashions. It shows an intellectual mastery that successfully transmutes materials little different from those of the previous plays into a work of art of a far more profound import, and yet more brilliant stage presence.

The character of Richard himself is obviously central to this new achievement, which to a large extent is the result of the simple fact that Richard *is* central. From Richard's opening "aria," we are left in no doubt where the focus of interest will lie, and whose point of view will color our view of the action. Edward may still be king at the start of the play and, at the end, the Tudors may supplant Richard; yet his career remains the dominant theme throughout, on the model of Marlowe's studies of monumental heroes in *Tamburlaine*, *The Jew of Malta*, and *Dr. Faustus*. By dexterously transposing their focal structure to the more elaborately realized setting and action of the English history play, Shakespeare shows an instinctive appreciation of the potentialities in the unusual treatment accorded by history to this last Yorkist king. For the Tudors who supplanted Richard III continued to rule in Shakespeare's time in the person of Elizabeth, and their version of their accession was necessarily the official one.

To most modern western artists (not to speak of critics), the need to write within the limits of such political requirements appears regrettable, the more so because the Tudors had systematically blackened their predecessor on the throne as a monster in human form. Works like the life of Richard III, ascribed (just possibly in error) to Sir Thomas More, not to mention Richard's comparable appearances in such full-scale histories as those of Polydore Vergil, Hall, and Holinshed, all established him in popular imagination as the epitome of every vice that had afflicted English society during the Wars of the Roses. This in itself provided Shakespeare with that heightening of personality that drama favors, and to which the earlier plays had already tended, in such characters as Joan, Margaret, Suffolk, and Cade. But Shakespeare is not content merely with a political caricature in this form. From Marlowe's Jew, Richard acquires that rationale of the ambitious villain that the Elizabethans (in default of an accurate and popularly accessible translation) made of Machiavelli's thought. Richard's long soliloquy in *Henry VI, Part 3* (III.ii.124ff.), along with his others in *Richard III*, establish him as the essence of Renaissance political ruthlessness.

But if Richard is both in harmony with Tudor myth, and motivated by a fashionable (if now incredible) logic, his role is not conceived out of harmony with the traditions of the theater for which it was written. The allegorical tendencies of the morality and polemical chronicle plays developed figures whose personality approximated to the extravagance of Shakespeare's Richard—a fact that is stressed by many of Richard's own remarks. He consciously alludes to the style of the cunning tempters in the morality tradition in an aside following an ambiguous remark:

> Thus, like the formal vice, Iniquity,
> I moralize two meanings in one word.
> (III.i.82–3)

Earlier in the play, he went back to the even older tradition of the mystery plays with their religious themes and Biblical figures—just as Marlowe did with his angels and devils in *Dr. Faustus*. After striking a hypocritically pious attitude, Richard soliloquizes:

> And thus I clothe my naked villany
> With old odd ends stolen out of holy writ;
> And seem a saint, when most I play the devil.
> (I.iii.336–8)

Such explicit allusions reveal the deliberateness of Shakespeare's assimilation of the play to the older dramatic tradition.

Yet Richard remains for most of us an extremely modern character, one that lends itself to modern psychological analysis both in terms of the character himself, and in his relation to the audience. The issue of Richard's deformity (of which there is no trace in the realistic portrait of the historical Richard in the National Portrait Gallery) is a fashionable theme of psychological debate. Shakespeare, wisely alert to the need for at least a surface plausibility of motivation, uses several soliloquies to make Richard's deformity the key to his compensatory ruth-

lessness. He shows the understandable hostility of the cripple for his more happily endowed contemporaries:

> But I, that am curtail'd of this fair proportion,
> Cheated of feature by dissembling nature,
> Deform'd, unfinish'd, sent before my time
> Into this breathing world, scarce half made up,
> And that so lamely and unfashionable
> That dogs bark at me as I halt by them;
> Why, I, in this weak piping time of peace,
> Have no delight to pass away the time,
> Unless to spy my shadow in the sun
> And descant on my own deformity:
> And therefore, since I cannot prove a lover,
> To entertain these fair well-spoken days,
> I am determined to prove a villain.
>   (I.i.18–30)

Yet if we consider the logic of other characters in the
play, this self-interpretation is the merest rationalization.
Far from being the cause of Richard's villainy, his deformity would, to many medieval and renaissance minds, be the
symptom of it—like the devil's cloven hoof and his other
bestial trappings. Henry VI certainly sees Richard's deformity as symbolic:

> Thy mother felt more than a mother's pain,
> And yet brought forth less than a mother's hope,
> To wit, an indigested and deformed lump,
> Not like the fruit of such a goodly tree.
> Teeth hadst thou in thy head when thou wast born,
> To signify thou camest to bite the world.
>   (3HVI, V.vi.49–54)

In general Richard appears—in the mouths of others as
well as in his own description—as evil by instinct, not by
breeding; however plausible his expressed motivations for
the decline into viciousness, Richard is not presented as a
case-history of such a decline, as is Macbeth or Othello.
He appears from his birth to be a more or less diabolical
personality. That is his power—and his charm.

For Richard surpasses any earlier Shakespearean character in hypnotic power. To a large extent, this arises from
his capacity both to grasp fully his own evil nature, and
to act in accordance with it, untrammeled by such hesita-
tions and regrets as beset a character like Macbeth. Yet
Richard's cheerful and efficient villainy, far from repelling
the audience, delights it. This confidence in the audience's
response shows Shakespeare's power to break through the
crust of rationalizing moral prejudice and respect for
decorum to the disruptive inner springs of human motivation. Richard has the fascination of the superman—intel-
ligent, witty, superior to human limitations and virtues.
More seriously, he is the focus for the vicarious release of
all the repressed resentments and desires that men share in
a complex, organized society—and which we have seen
disastrously liberated in the English aristocrats of Shakespeare's earlier studies of the Wars of the Roses. Richard
has thus an extraordinarily cathartic role, which largely
explains the play's enduring popularity: we enjoy his
virtuosity, share his contempt for his fellows' insensitivity,
and shiver with delight at his macabre humor. In a memorable (if nominally unhistorical) scene he wins Lady
Anne, and we derive a vicarious satisfaction from his
superiority to sentiment, as he adds, "I'll have her; but I
will not keep her long." When Buckingham wonders
what to do with Hastings, we share the thrill of un-
bridled authority on hearing Richard's Alexandrine solution, "Chop off his head, man!"; and we may even giggle,
a little nervously, when the unfortunate Hastings is told:

> Dispatch, my lord; the duke would be at dinner:
> Make a short shrift; he longs to see your head.
> (III.iv.96–7)

Above all we sympathize with Richard's contempt for
cant and superstition, triumphantly illustrated by his refusal to be discountenanced by the lack of sunshine before
his last battle:

Not shine today! Why what is that to me
More than to Richmond? for the selfsame heaven
That frowns on me looks sadly upon him.

(V.iii.285–7)

Richard's ability to rise above the necessities of compromise must fascinate all those who feel the burden of
apparently inescapable decorum and constraint that civili-
zation imposes on our basic instincts. His career allows
us an initially triumphant indulgence in vicious wish-
fulfillment of a kind that was unrecognized by Aristotle,
yet is socially purgative in his sense.

Yet if a work of art is to be more than a sociological
phenomenon, it must have some motivating principle that
is superior to providing vicarious satisfaction for primitive
impulses. In fact, one may wonder whether the character
of Richard is not given false prominence because of the
almost pathological excitement he arouses. It might be
considered a serious criticism of Richard as a character in
a history play to say that not only is he a gross misrepre-
sentation of an historical person who was no worse (and
possibly even a little better) than his contemporaries, but
also that his personality is completely incredible in a way
that even the personalities of Joan, Margaret, or Cade are
not. One may begin to wonder whether the play can
properly be called a history play at all; once this question
is raised, it becomes clear that the play gains enormously
from consideration as a study in an older form, as the
morality play that Richard's occasional asides seem to
make it. If anything, the other characters see their world
more clearly than does Richard as the medieval one into
which both metaphysical evil and metaphysical good enter
freely and intelligibly.

This view is conspicuously characteristic of Queen
Margaret, whose unpredictable but plausible transmutation
from ambitious sentimentalist to avenging angel is one of
the most brilliant strokes of character development in
Shakespeare. Margaret haunts the action of *Richard III*,
her rhetorical vehemence and utter acceptance of the

medieval cosmic order making her a worthy spiritual antagonist of Richard. To her question:

> Can curses pierce the clouds and enter heaven?
> (I.iii.195)

she later makes her own emphatic reply:

> I'll not believe but they ascend the sky,
> And there awake God's gentle-sleeping peace.
> (I.iii.287-8)

Even Richard seems somewhat intimidated by the volcanic prophecies she launches at him and attempts to turn them aside by a trick (I.iii.234ff.). As for the others whom she foredooms, their initial indifference and skepticism is shattered by the fulfillment of her predictions in disturbingly precise detail. As Rivers, Vaughan, and Grey are led to execution, Grey suddenly realizes:

> Now Margaret's curse is fall'n upon our heads
> For standing by when Richard stabb'd her son.
> (III.iii.15-16)

Rivers assents and intensifies the other predictions made by Margaret:

> Then cursed she Hastings, then cursed she Buckingham,
> Then cursed she Richard. O, remember, God,
> To hear her prayers for them, as now for us!
> (III.iii.17-19)

And in the very next scene it is Hastings who meets his doom, with a recognition of its origins that resembles that of the earlier victims:

> O Margaret, Margaret, now thy heavy curse
> Is lighted on poor Hastings' wretched head!
> (III.iv.94-5)

No wonder that Margaret's role is a major part of the tetralogy: now she lurks in the wings like the vengeful ghost in *The Spanish Tragedy*, but far more significantly. Her choric utterances have an intensity that is derived from her intimate involvement in the fates of those over whose demise she presides. Well may she gloat:

> So, now prosperity begins to mellow
> And drop into the rotten mouth of death.
> Here in these confines have I slyly lurk'd,
> To watch the waning of mine adversaries.
> A dire induction am I witness to,
> And will to France, hoping the consequence
> Will prove as bitter, black, and tragical.
> (IV.iv.1–7)

But before she goes she summarizes the realization of her forecasts for her successor, Queen Elizabeth, mother to the young princes who have been murdered in the Tower:

> Where is thy husband now? where be thy brothers?
> Where are thy children? Wherein dost thou joy?
> Who sues to thee and cries "God save the queen"?
> (IV.iv.92–4)

After the success of her anticipations, she may well apologize to the widowed Duchess of York:

> Bear with me: I am hungry for revenge,
> And now I cloy me with beholding it.
> (IV.iv.61–2)

Even after her final departure, her agency seems effective. Act V begins memorably with the final downfall of Richard's tool Buckingham, who, finding that the day of his execution is All-Souls' Day, exclaims:

> Why then All-Souls' Day is my body's doomsday.
> This is the day that in King Edward's time,
> I wish'd might fall on me, when I was found
> False to his children or his wife's allies; . . .
> That high All-Seer that I dallied with
> Hath turn'd my feigned prayer on my head
> And given in earnest what I begg'd in jest. . . .
> Now Margaret's curse is fallen upon my head;
> "When he," quoth she, "shall split thy heart with sorrow,
> Remember Margaret was a prophetess."
> (V.i.12–15,20–2,25–7)

Buckingham's speech epitomizes the powerful medieval rhythm of the play's action, where a chance word or a hasty promise is inescapably loaded with metaphysical enforcements, even when Margaret herself is not involved. One remembers how Lady Anne, in cursing Richard, unconsciously extends her malediction to herself when she wishes evil on any wife he marries—as she herself recalls:

> This was my wish: "Be thou," quoth I, "accursed,
> For making me so young so old a widow!
> And when thou wed'st, let sorrow haunt thy bed;
> And be thy wife—if any be so mad—
> As miserable by the life of thee
> As thou hast made me by my dear lord's death!"
> Lo, ere I can repeat this curse again,
> Even in so short a space, my woman's heart
> Grossly grew captive to his honey words
> And proved the subject of my own soul's curse.
>
> (IV.i.72–81)

Here one sees a virtuosity of dramatic irony comparable to that which provides the structure of Sophocles' *Oedipus Rex*.

In fact, from the start this rhythm is firmly illustrated by the downfall and execution of Clarence, with which the opening phases of the play are chiefly concerned. The long scene before his execution is loaded with ironies and calculated correspondences from the very opening lines, which establish a pathetic resolution to the problem of Clarence's insomnia. The "ghastly dreams" resulting from his misdeeds are such:

> That, as I am a Christian faithful man,
> I would not spend another such a night,
> Though 'twere to buy a world of happy days.
>
> (I.iv.4–6)

His desires are, of course, exactly realized, because no sooner does he fall asleep again than he is handed over to his murderers, whose resolution to kill him is fortified against his appeal to God's laws by the fact that he himself has broken them. They do not fear his threat of God's vengeance, because they feel they are the agents of it.

> And that same vengeance doth he hurl on thee
> For false forswearing and for murder too:
> Thou didst receive the holy sacrament,
> To fight in quarrel of the house of Lancaster.
>
> (I.iv.206–9)

Clarence has lost the moral initiative and thus his guilt dooms him as plausibly, in practical terms, as any external medieval cosmic rhythm might have required.

Still, if we can perceive the purely circumstantial logic of the disasters befalling such victims, Richard's agency does remain significant. He and Margaret are the two poles between which the body of the play revolves, and her estimate of his nature remains the most valuable in the play. If she is an avenging angel in intent, he is God's scourge of man's villainy in practice. As Margaret perceives:

> Richard yet lives, hell's black intelligencer,
> Only reserved their factor, to buy souls
> And send them thither.
>
> (IV.iv.71–3)

Richard functions, for her, as an agent of the Devil— buying up lost souls, and sending them to hell; and this is no idle conceit of a lunatic mind (rather, her perceptions are heightened by suffering, in the manner that Aeschylus had already indicated in his great trilogy). Many times Richard is identified as a "cacodemon," a "devil"; a careful study of the evolution of the play makes it clear that this is in fact his essential role in its structure. And since a diabolical spirit is inflexible by nature and cannot properly be the essential subject of drama (any more than Satan can be the hero of *Paradise Lost*), it becomes necessary to reshape our view of the play, in order to see that the real evolution of dynamic action lies outside Richard. It lies in the minds of the English men and women whom he appears to betray.

Far from being simply a Marlovian study of egotistic monomania in a single character, the play is better seen as a study of the impact of that monomania on a whole series of individuals. This inner structure of *Richard III* requires it to be grouped with such a sequence of moralized histories as the *Mirror for Magistrates;* if the play is seen as a series of brilliant vignettes, cleverly harmonized and with a cumulative impact, then it becomes less implausible, and Richard's function wholly realistic and intelligible. For Richard rarely functions as a discrete human entity; he is far more the insinuating voice of that manic egotism and greed that seemed to govern England throughout the Wars of the Roses. Each scene in which he impinges on the consciousness of others is to a large degree a psycho-machia like that in the morality plays, in which we see symbolized (but not fictionalized) the mental processes that bring about the historical events with which the play deals.

If we see Richard as a catalyst, or better still as a re-flection, of the latent will and the greedy self-deception of those with whom he has dealings, many curious scenes become more meaningful. Perhaps the most conspicuous of these is the extraordinary second scene of the play in which Richard manages to win the favor of the woman whose husband he has murdered. Lady Anne is a some-what conventional young woman, as her stilted laments over the bier of Henry VI reveal—they are full of paral-lelisms, repetitions and extravagance. Into this solemn rhythm Richard breaks brusquely, like an unchaste thought; and Lady Anne identifies him melodramatically, yet with unconscious exactness, as a "minister of hell," a "foul devil." She soon finds this very flamboyance of hers a weakness, since it allows her opponent to strike a plau-sible attitude of moderation and suave religiosity once his energy has broken through her endless lament. Richard shows all the skill of the virtuoso in excuses such as modern psychiatry ascribes to the rationalizations of pathological desires. His very effrontery and sophistication blunt opposition, once one deigns to argue with him on the same plane. When Anne exclaims with wonder "when devils tell the truth," Richard sharply ripostes:

More wonderful when angels are so angry.
Vouchsafe, divine perfection of a woman,
Of these supposed evils to give me leave,
By circumstance, but to acquit myself.
(I.ii.74–7)

Here, as Iago is so often, Richard is nominally in the right. Anne's vehemence does her cause no service, and her desire for caustic ripostes simply enables Richard's macabre humor to deflate her outbursts. When she asserts that Henry VI is in heaven, Richard drily responds:

Let him thank me, that holp to send him thither;
For he was fitter for that place than earth.
(I.ii.107–8)

No excuse for murder, the reply still has enough wit and acid truth to sustain the speaker's initiative, and allow him —after the climactic shock of proposing himself as Anne's lover—to affect to restore decorum:

But, gentle Lady Anne,
To leave this keen encounter of our wits,
And fall into a slower method:
Is not the causer of the timeless deaths
Of these Plantagenets, Henry and Edward,
As blameful as the executioner?
(I.ii.114–19)

The question again is too fair to permit easy effective answer, and thus allows Richard's key argument to be brought into play unhindered:

Your beauty was the cause of that effect;
Your beauty, which did haunt me in my sleep
To undertake the death of all the world,
So I might live one hour in your sweet bosom.
(I.ii.121–4)

The argument is objectively negligible. Nevertheless, it is emotionally potent, and not unsurprisingly it is therefore at least hypothetically entertained by Anne when she accepts the fact of her own charm:

> If I thought that, I tell thee, homicide,
> These nails should rend that beauty from my cheeks.
> (I.ii.125–6)

She has now clearly lost the initiative: Richard's flashing intellect and protean personality defy her ability to sustain her early monomanic note effectively. He rapidly reverses their roles. Her bitter act of spitting on him allows him to usurp her suffering role and to leave her now in a wounding posture:

> Those eyes of thine from mine have drawn salt tears,
> Shamed their aspect with store of childish drops:
> These eyes, which never shed remorseful tear,
> No, when my father York and Edward wept,
> To hear the piteous moan that Rutland made
> When black-faced Clifford shook his sword at him;
> Nor when thy warlike father, like a child,
> Told the sad story of my father's death,
> And twenty times made pause to sob and weep.
> (I.ii.156–64)

The allusion to his own bereavement and to her father, once the Yorkists' ally, further complicate the emotional situation, and in this context Richard is able to achieve his climactic stroke—the shattering of her attitude by demonstrating its merely rhetorical character:

> Teach not thy lips such scorn, for they were made
> For kissing, lady, not for such contempt.
> If thy revengeful heart cannot forgive,
> Lo, here I lend thee this sharp-pointed sword;
> Which if thou please to hide in this true bosom,
> And let the soul forth that adoreth thee,
> I lay it naked to the deadly stroke.
> (I.ii.172–8)

For all her curses Anne cannot, in this context of emotional confusion, find the authority to act as decisively as she has spoken. More moderation earlier would have made such a challenge meaningless now, but once she has admitted her earlier extravagance, Richard forces her back relentlessly, even offering to kill himself now if she asks it; and when she insists that she already has, his argument is disarmingly accurate:

> Tush, that was in thy rage:
> Speak it again, and, even with the word,
> That hand, which, for thy love did kill thy love,
> Shall, for thy love, kill a far truer love;
> To both their deaths thou shalt be accessary.
>
> (I.ii.188–92)

Flattered by the thought that their beauty could drive men to crime, both Isabella (in *Measure for Measure*) and Anne can pardon that crime; but Isabella has a far subtler character than Anne, whose susceptibility to facile rhetoric has already appeared in her opening florid lament. The parallel in the early career of Margaret, with her courtship by Suffolk's facile eloquence, presents a model for what is presented in condensed form in Anne's far briefer career as Richard's wife and queen. Yet Anne's deception by Richard is not merely episodic; it is the norm for all but the most hardened judges (like Margaret) in the play. Most seriously of all, it is the norm for the readers and audience also.

The *coup de théâtre* by which Richard wins Anne establishes us also as his victims, for if intellectually we see a little deeper into him than she does, we are still prone to view his victims from his own merciless perspective, at least unconsciously. We laugh at his macabre jokes and connive in his plots by enjoying his sardonic asides and soliloquies. There is surely also a poetic truth in Richard's seduction of Anne that is related to her historical nature: she must have married the real Richard at least in part from the desire to find any plausible refuge from the anarchy of the times, even if it were in the arms of a lover who might technically be her enemy (the first husband she lost having been one in form only).

Whatever its roots in history, this second scene of the play establishes the rhetorical seductiveness by which evil insinuates itself—if anything more easily into the hearts of those who are to be most afflicted by its consequences. And the play takes its course through the exposition and evaluation of those states of mind in which evil is conceived, accepted, and expiated. This, rather than any logical historical process, governs the sequence of events in the plot. Anne's reversal of feeling is followed first by the contrasting rigor of Margaret's denunciation of Richard, and then by a detailed study, in Clarence's nightmare sequence in the Tower, of the fate of those like Anne and Clarence, who switch allegiances on the selfish impulse of the moment. This concern with studying fatal states of mind explains and justifies the otherwise somewhat extraneous poetry of the dream sequence. It also explains the extraordinary depth in which the characters of Clarence's two murderers are developed. There is a typical Shakespearean irony in that the murderers' debate is a reverse image of that process of moral self-clarification that all Richard's victims initially fail to achieve. The murderers are, of course, also his victims, betrayed into the commission of crime by their greed; yet they remain confusedly aware of the issues. The second murderer in particular raises the issue of responsibility in a way conspicuously ignored by the English aristocracy for the most part in the tetralogy. He says, when asked by his companion "What, art thou afraid?":

> Not to kill him, having a warrant for it; but to be damned for killing him, from which no warrant can defend us.

> (I.iv.112–14)

But rapidly the balance is reversed and he denounces that guide to action that is so rarely consulted by the characters in the play—conscience. In terms anticipating Hamlet, he calls it:

> . . . a dangerous thing: it makes a man a coward: a man cannot steal, but it accuseth him; he cannot swear, but it checks him; he cannot lie with his neighbour's wife, but it detects him; 'tis a blushing shamefast spirit that mutinies in a man's bosom; it fills one full of obstacles. . . . Every man that means to live well endeavours to trust to himself and to live without it.
>
> (I.iv.137–42,145–7)

The tensions described here are conspicuously lacking in almost all the characters in the play—until it is too late to profit from them. Ironically, in persuading his companion to throw off the promptings of conscience, the speaker advises his companion to treat it like an evil spirit:

> Take the devil in thy mind, and believe him not: he would insinuate with thee but to make thee sigh.
>
> (I.iv.151–3)

Their subsequent informal trial of Clarence before they assassinate him only serves to strengthen the audience's sense of the nature of moral action. Despite Clarence's ultimate loss of initiative because of his own guilt, the scene reaches a peak in Clarence's speech on the nature of individual human responsibility, which must be primary, whatever the force of authority:

> Erroneous vassal! the great King of kings
> Hath in the tables of his law commanded
> That thou shalt do no murder: and wilt thou, then,
> Spurn at his edict and fulfil a man's?
> Take heed; for he holds vengeance in his hands,
> To turn upon their heads that break his law.
>
> (I.iv.200–5)

One of Clarence's later, desperate exclamations, "Not to relent is beastly, savage, devilish" rings on into the next scene, where the news of his death stuns the assembled court, to be followed—schematically, yet abruptly—by

Derby's plea for mercy to a servant who slew a gentle-man. The explosion of King Edward's nerves at the dis-turbing juxtaposition of this plea with the fact of his own brother's death is one of the most memorable speeches of the play:

> Have I a tongue to doom my brother's death
> And shall the same give pardon to a slave?
> My brother slew no man; his fault was thought,
> And yet his punishment was cruel death.
> Who sued to me for him? who, in my rage,
> Kneel'd at my feet, and bade me be advised?
> Who spake of brotherhood? who spake of love? . . .
> But when your carters or your waiting-vassals
> Have done a drunken slaughter, and defaced
> The precious image of our dear Redeemer,
> You straight are on your knees for pardon, pardon;
> And I, unjustly too, must grant you:
> But for my brother not a man would speak,
> Nor I, ungracious, speak unto myself
> For him, poor soul.
> (II.i.102–8,121–8)

Here at least is the tragic realization that has eluded so many characters in the three parts of Henry VI. Edward is many steps closer to the heroic self-recognition that is to mark such characters as Othello and Lear when they make comparable mistakes.

But if Edward's recognition of his fault is classic, the most perfect example of the cycle of *hubris* lies in the study of Hastings, whose rise and fall requires only two swift scenes, laden with such omens as his vindictive yet unconsciously self-directed comment on the death of his enemies Rivers, Vaughan, and Grey:

> . . . so 'twill do
> With some men else, who think themselves as safe
> As thou and I.
> (III.ii.67–9)

The dramatic irony of Hastings' misestimation of Richard is in a similar vein, the absolute mistaking of the situation having clearly a schematic rather than a psychological interest:

> I think there's never a man in Christendom
> That can less hide his love or hate than he;
> For by his face straight shall you know his heart.
> (III.iv.53–5)

This failure in discrimination is a uniform characteristic of all Richard's victims. Rivers earlier had praised Richard's moderation in his censure of Clarence's murderers, not realizing that Richard was carefully taking into account his own part in the assassination.

This kind of lucidity on Richard's part is another superhuman characteristic of his mind; it stands in interesting contrast to the apparently analogous character of Buckingham, who is the most sustained conventional character study in the play. Buckingham shows in practical, historical operation all those qualities that are more symbolically epitomized in Richard. It is interesting to note that the deluded initiative of Hastings finds an analogy in the initiatory role that Buckingham assumes, unaware of Richard's ironic contempt at this presupposition of superior insight:

> My other self, my counsel's consistory,
> My oracle, my prophet! My dear cousin,
> I, like a child, will go by thy direction.
> (II.ii.151–3)

The relationship with Buckingham in its early phases well illustrates the essentially catalytic role that Richard usually plays whenever he impinges on the moral responsibility of others. He has power over the bodies of those around him, but not over their wills; it is with their own assent that he destroys them morally, allowing their weaknesses scope rather than enforcing his own personality upon them. Buckingham is quite indignant at the idea that Richard would need to teach him duplicity:

Tut, I can counterfeit the deep tragedian;
Speak and look back, and pry on every side,
Tremble and start at wagging of a straw,
Intending deep suspicion. . . .
                    (III.v.5–8)

It is all the more interesting, therefore, to note that the
relationship between Richard and Buckingham evolves far
more than any of the others. Buckingham arrives at his
awareness at an earlier phase of his career than the last
fatal moments when self-knowledge came to Hastings and
the others. One remembers that he had initially been sufficiently uncompromised to be favored by Queen Margaret,
and his hesitation to accept Richard's first proposition
during the course of their relationship—to murder the
princes in the Tower—is a turning point in the play.
Hitherto, not unlike the audience, Buckingham has enjoyed Richard's wit, and taken advantage of the political
finesse it fosters; at this point, however, neither Buckingham nor the audience can find any delight in such a
massacre of innocents—an act of diabolical rather than
human proportions. There is weight in the severing of
relations by Richard:

The deep-revolving witty Buckingham
No more shall be the neighbour to my counsel:
Hath he so long held out with me untired,
And stops he now for breath?
                    (IV.ii.42–5)

However, Richard's momentum is like that of human
ambition—it flags when the goal is reached, in this case
the Crown of England. Thereafter, Buckingham's departure marks the conclusion of one major phase of
Richard's role as epitome of the magnetic, dark passion of
egotism. From about this point on, Shakespeare concerns
himself with the negative, declining aspects of this element
of Richard's personality. Richard is essentially an abstract
of certain human traits; in that sense, the logic of his fall

is only superficially naturalistic. In the earlier parts of the play, Shakespeare has chosen to show the ruthless efficiency of egotism. To give the sequence harmony with the overall rhythm of the Wheel of Fortune in the second part he illustrates the negative phases of egotism, its self-destructive character. In the scene before Buckingham's instinctive revulsion, Lady Anne gives a firm indication of the subconscious penalties that are associated with Richard's conscious virtuosity, whose demands undermine his inward stability:

> For never yet one hour in his bed
> Have I enjoyed the golden dew of sleep,
> But have been waked by his timorous dreams.
> (IV.i.83–5)

In harmony with this revelation, the scene immediately following Buckingham's revulsion starts with Tyrrel's pathetic description of the murder of Richard's innocent victims in the Tower—a description carefully calculated to alienate the audience's sympathy from Richard, and to lessen their delight in his wit, which is thereafter no longer allowed the same virtuosity. His wife's death is revealed with parenthetic and humorless casualness:

> And Anne my wife hath bid the world good night.
> (IV.iii.39)

and the next scene gathers a symbolic triad of affronted women: Queen Margaret, Queen Elizabeth, and the Duchess of York. These three bereaved mothers form an archetypal triad like Macbeth's witches—except that Richard's agency crystallizes the outraged femininity of mothers and wives arrayed against him, while in *Macbeth* what man's evil calls out is an answering evil in nature.

Richard's confrontation by his mother and Queen Elizabeth sets the seal on his downward course. His mother's powerful curse is followed by the attempt to win Queen Elizabeth's daughter, a scene as joyless as the earlier courtship of Anne was vivacious and dashing. Not only does Elizabeth fail to live up to Richard's expectations, but his loss of enthusiasm and poise causes him soon after to chide Catesby for not leaving with a message that Richard has actually forgotten to give him, and later Richard becomes so upset by bad news that he even strikes the innocent bearer of the news. Just before the battle Richard asks for wine to revive his jaded spirit, confessing:

> I have not that alacrity of spirit,
> Nor cheer of mind, that I was wont to have.
>
> (V.iii.73-4)

This loss of energy is not shown in terms of Richard's conscience, as with Macbeth's, but externally, as if by metaphysical requirement. Richard's dream epitomizes this sense of an external, fated rhythm in the play. The victims of Richard are massed ritually in a counterpoint of curses on Richard and blessings on Richmond.

This scene comes as a kind of climax to the incantatory, almost ecclesiastical tone, and medieval movement of the play's plot. In many ways, it is Shakespeare's most medieval play in its texture, structure, and attitudes. Despite the sequence of vignettes of human fallibility, *Richard III* progresses conceptually and dogmatically, not psychologically and pragmatically. Perhaps the strongest illustration of this lies in Richard's extraordinary speech when he wakes from his nightmare. There is no passion in Richard's self-analysis, merely paradoxical rhetoric:

> What do I fear? myself? there's none else by:
> Richard loves Richard; that is, I am I.
> Is there a murderer here? No. Yes, I am.
> Then fly. What, from myself? Great reason why:
> Lest I revenge. What, myself upon myself?
> Alack, I love myself. Wherefore? for any good
> That I myself have done unto myself?
> O, no! alas, I rather hate myself
> For hateful deeds committed by myself.
>
> (V.iii.182-90)

He coldly determines that even he finds "in myself no pity to myself." A more analytic estimate of the situation could hardly have been provided by a medieval theologian.

If then *Richard III* is a triumph dramatically through its humorous, Machiavellian villain-hero, its achievements are nevertheless not those of the history play. It derives from and returns to the world of myth: the larger-than-life whose functions are schematic, not compromised by the ambiguities and confusions that are near the heart of all political activity. The superiority of *Richard III* over *Henry VI* is obtained at the expense of the genre of the history play rather than by deriving strength from it, which may explain why there seems to be such a letdown from *Richard III* to *King John*. The contrast between the omnipotent villain-hero of the earlier play and the wretched villain-king of the second seems to be altogether in Richard's favor; yet there is little question which is the more historically plausible figure, and which play shows a greater concern with, and insight into political forces. Above all, it is *King John* that shows a greater inward dramatic tension. Richard may amuse us, but his genius is grimly contained by a structure of dogmatic sanctions. John is less absolute, more equivocating; the questions raised by his rule are far more modern than those posed by Richard's.

II

KING JOHN

🐦 *King John*

THE CENTRAL THEME of *King John* is
brought forward in one of Richard's speeches. When
Richard is informed of Richmond's invasion and his claim
to the crown, Richard exclaims:

> Is the chair empty? is the sword unsway'd?
> Is the king dead? the empire unpossess'd?
> What heir of York is there alive but we?
> And who is England's king but great York's heir?
> Then, tell me, what doth he upon the sea?
>   (*RIII*, IV.iv.470–4)

At first sight these questions may seem merely rhetorical
in view of Richard's own murderous path to the crown
and his unequivocal villainy; but *King John* makes it clear
that for Shakespeare they are not rhetorical questions.
Their bearing on the actual coming to power of the
Tudors verges indeed on a dangerous questioning of the
nature of proper succession, which it was far safer and
more revealing to develop in relation to the remoter times
of *King John*. Again the issues anticipate the themes of
Hobbes' *Leviathan*: the nature of authority and the nature
of the sanctions that are properly invoked against it. Unlike *Henry VI*, which took a disturbingly pragmatic attitude to power—whoever rules, rules by right—*Richard III*
assumed that openly apparent evil in a ruler justifies his
overthrow. To a modern reader, the question might seem
to be answered rightly so. But the judgment is facile.

The English genius has tended to favor evolution rather than revolution as the best solution to bad government. For this theme, the reign of King John was an ideal subject, the more so in that Shakespeare's subtly balanced mind perceived that John's reign provided the occasion for an ambiguity of contemporary interpretation that allowed a freedom of judgment denied him in the too recent history of the Tudors' predecessor. John was (and usually still is) considered to be a poor king, forced reluctantly to accept the *Magna Carta*, which chiefly vindicated the barons' feudal privileges and their independence of central authority; he was also tainted with similar associations to those involving Richard III, being apparently a usurper and the murderer of the innocent rightful heir, Prince Arthur. Further, his defiance of the church affronted orthodox Catholic opinions at least as late as the Tudors' humanist historian, Polydore Vergil. Nevertheless, it was precisely this defiance of Italianate papal authority that finally drew the Tudors closest to him. Since they shared his desire to destroy the papal power of intervention in English political affairs, it is not surprising that John often appears in a more favorable light from the time of Bishop John Bale's morality *King John* (c. 1540), down to the two-part anonymous chronicle play on which Shakespeare's history is based.

Shakespeare's play is not popular; it is not often performed, probably because of the emotional problem presented to an audience by the character of its central figure, John himself. Yet it is just this ambivalence of response (a minor-key version of what we feel for Richard III) that constitutes the central political and theatrical interest of the play. This lies in the creative tension of two incompatible sets of values: dislike of John as a man, and recognition of the substantial fact of his kingship. Shakespeare's strategy in securing the parity of these issues appears in the opening scene, where English sovereignty is brusquely called into question by the French ambassador. Whatever an English audience might feel about John, there would be no doubt of the offensiveness to patriotism of Chatillon's imperiousness:

> Philip of France, in right and true behalf
> Of thy deceased brother Geffrey's son,
> Arthur Plantagenet, lays most lawful claim
> To this fair island and the territories,
> To Ireland, Poictiers, Anjou, Touraine, Maine.
> (I.i.7–11)

John's answer is polite and firm, based on his sense of the resources he possesses:

> Our strong possession and our right for us.
> (I.i.39)

His mother drily revises the estimate:

> Your strong possession much more than your right,
> Or else it must go wrong with you and me:
> So much my conscience whispers in your ear,
> Which none but heaven and you and I shall hear.
> (I.i.40–3)

She highlights the difference between John and Richard III by her regrets over John's failure to avert conflict with the French king. Subtler policies would have kept Constance and her son Arthur in England, at John's disposition:

> This might have been prevented and made whole
> With very easy arguments of love,
> Which now the manage of two kingdoms must
> With fearful bloody issue arbitrate.
> (I.i.35–8)

In these few lines Shakespeare establishes as the central issue not so much the nature of John himself but his role as King of England. It is this theme alone that explains the unexpected change of direction in the opening scene, which now continues to devote itself to the fortunes of Philip, the bastard son of Richard Cœur-de-Lion. The analogies between Philip and John are as interesting as the contrasts between them. Both are significantly indebted to their mothers—John for counsel from Queen Elinor, who effectively buttresses his succession to her dead elder son, Richard I (Cœur-de-Lion); Philip for the dynamic temperament he inherits from his father, the same Richard, whose magnetic charm had seduced his mother during her husband's absence. More formally speaking, both stand in dubious relation to their inheritances: the claim of each is legally questioned by a weaker but theoretically better justified claimant. However, while Philip, confidently trusting to fortune and his headlong personality, gives up his patrimony, John cannily maintains his position on the throne. These opposite reactions reflect not only the personalities involved, but also the diversity of the issues: Philip's surrender of his private inheritance involves shame to his mother, but advantage to the state, to whose service he dedicates himself. If John had as abruptly surrendered England, that state would itself have collapsed and become merely a protectorate of France. While Philip, the individual, may act both legalistically and extravagantly without danger, John's position is hedged by political and diplomatic considerations that complicate his moral and temperamental concerns as an individual.

It may be said that despite their diverse responses to nominally similar circumstances both men are realists. There are unmistakable affinities between them. They are both conspicuously heirs to Richard I, John inheriting his kingdom, and Philip his individualism and his dynamic temperament. John and his mother feel an instinctive attraction to this "madcap" sent them by heaven (I.i.84ff.); John decides that he is "a good blunt fellow," whose attributes are "perfect Richard," and Elinor agrees. Sharing no less fully in the various striking attributes of Shakespeare's Richard III, as well as in those of the earlier Richard, this strange triumvirate thereafter manages to dominate England far more realistically than the superman of the earlier history play. John has his villainous, corrupt values, without that finesse with which they are, after all, incompatible; Elinor has Richard's political slyness and finesse, but without his humor and wit; the Bastard has Richard's vivacity and verbal energy, larger than life no doubt, but more suitable for an incidental role with symbolic overtones than for such a central, historically defined character as Richard III or John. Philip follows the more amusing parts of Richard's pattern of behavior from the start, boldly undercutting convention and affectation. Raised to knighthood, he soliloquizes, like Richard in his prologue, on the follies of his contemporaries, rising rapidly to Richard's choric power of generalization and self-analysis:

> But this is worshipful society
> And fits a mounting spirit like myself,
> For he is but a bastard to the time
> That doth not smack of observation;
> And so am I, whether I smack or no;
> And not alone in habit and device,
> Exterior form, outward accoutrement,
> But from the inward motion to deliver
> Sweet, sweet, sweet poison for the age's tooth:
> Which, though I will not practise to deceive,
> Yet, to avoid deceit, I mean to learn;
> For it shall strew the footsteps of my rising.
>   (I.i.205–16)

This speech serves to establish the moral climate of the play, which is less given to extremes than *Richard III*. The earlier play had tended to hem in the virtuosity of the supremely bad, in the person of Richard, by a lattice-work of medieval ritual, in the form of curses and prophecies through which God's rigorous justice was vindicated. By contrast, in *King John* neither the very bad nor the very good appears clearly. The earlier age of John seems paradoxically to be far more modern and pragmatic, both in observing reality without metaphysical preconceptions and in following the dictates of expediency without looking beyond the satisfaction of egotistical desires. Thus the theological grounds for the behavior of the Papal Legate,

Cardinal Pandulph, are too logical and rarefied to make any sense to the inhabitants of this shoddy environment, and his perfectly consistent reversal of attitude to the "reformed" John appears rather quaint in the world of cynical political "deals" that is reflected in most of the play's action. At best, the various other leaders find it merely expedient to mask their innate greed for wealth and power under the guise of a crusade. To them, religion, the question of legal title to inheritance, and the familial relationships of mother and son (not to mention that of marriage itself) are mere nominal counters, which lend a formal decorum to crude political and diplomatic maneuvers.

Philip's cheerfully amoral attitude to his own illegitimacy is thus typical of his time except in so far as its cynical and egotistical foundation is not veiled by any of that uneasy hypocrisy that is characteristic of the titular leaders of society who appear in the play. Philip conserves a kind of integrity by this honesty, and with it the power of moral growth, which is denied to such unstable personalities as John himself. Philip's personality therefore serves in many ways to reflect the relatively detached consciousness of the audience: both have been matured and refined by observation of the events that impinge on his meteoric career. Carrying the audience along with him, Philip evolves out of the crude cynicism that is youth's first alternative to idealism into a resigned, even world-weary maturity that nevertheless proves compatible with an underlying vital impetus that survives from his youth. This still remaining idealism increasingly develops into a dauntless patriotism, with the result that Philip is the figure whose perspective governs an English audience's response to the play. By studying its action through his eyes, we shall therefore probably come closest to Shakespeare's own perspective, and to a sense of the political values that he is concerned to dramatize. It is these very subtle political values that lend to most of the characters in the play whatever complexity and fascination they may possess.

In Act II it is rapidly established that the character of
the English army resembles that of Philip the Bastard.
Chatillon describes John's entourage, and notes that there
comes

> With them a bastard of the king's deceased,
> And all the unsettled humours of the land,
> Rash, inconsiderate, fiery voluntaries,
> With ladies' faces and fierce dragons' spleens,
> Have sold their fortunes at their native homes,
> Bearing their birthrights proudly on their backs,
> To make a hazard of new fortunes here:
> In brief, a braver choice of dauntless spirits
> Than now the English bottoms have waft o'er
> Did never float upon the swelling tide
> To do offence and scath in Christendom.
>
> (II.i.65–75)

The reluctant admiration here is subtly blended with a
canting tone, which barely conceals the French envy at
the appearance of an army marching against them that is
comparable in spirit to that with which the French themselves had hoped to invade England. Thereafter, John's
dry and practical tone is more in harmony with the basic
attitudes of both sides than are King Philip's solemn
protestations that "England we love" (II.i.91), and that
only a sense of moral outrage at the violation of legitimate
succession governs his support of Arthur and his challenge
to the English. John coolly inquires:

> From whom hast thou this great commission, France,
> To draw my answer from thy articles?
>
> (II.i.110–11)

To the French king's reply:

> From that supernal judge, that stirs good thoughts
> In any breast of strong authority,
> To look into the blots and stains of right:
> That judge hath made me guardian to this boy:

Under whose warrant I impeach thy wrong
And by whose help I mean to chastise it.
(II.i.112–17)

John's skeptical rejoinder: "Alack, thou dost usurp authority," again proves truer to the actual circumstances of
their encounter, as the remaining, almost grotesque action
of this scene startingly illustrates. Not only do Elinor and
Constance fall from the high, canting tone of the French
king into scurrilous abuse of each other's inchastity (to the
shame of Arthur), but the citizens of Angiers dramatize
the pragmatic attitudes invited by the play's action, in re-
fusing to accept in advance either authority, feeling that
"he that proves the king" must first have met the test by
defeating the other's army (II.i.270ff.).

At this point, the Bastard studies the whole situation
with the fascinated detachment of a political scientist like
Machiavelli, concerned only to examine the quirks of
kingly temper. After the first drawn encounter, he even
spurs on the battle, as one might stir up an anthill, purely
out of curiosity:

Ha, majesty! how high thy glory towers
When the rich blood of kings is set on fire!
O, now doth Death line his dead chaps with steel;
The swords of soldiers are his teeth, his fangs
And now he feasts, mousing the flesh of men,
In undetermined differences of kings.
Why stand these royal fronts amazed thus?
Cry, 'havoc!' kings; back to the stained field,
You equal potents, fiery kindled spirits!
Then let confusion of one part confirm
The other's peace; till then, blows, blood and death!
(II.i.350–60)

There is the same exuberant irony in this deadly advice
as Swift later deploys in his *Modest Proposal*. Meanwhile,
the citizens of Angiers persist in identifying the legal king
by the military supremacy that each side claims, as yet
without justification. For, as the citizens note of the rival
assertions:

A greater power than we denies all this;
And till it be undoubted, we do lock
Our former scruple in our strong-barr'd gates;
King'd of our fears, until our fears, resolved,
Be by some certain king purged and deposed.

(II.i.368–72)

This utterly cynical (or utterly pragmatic) attitude to
the legality of authority is perfectly in harmony with
Hobbes' view that the effective wielding of authority is
the validation of its possession. Like many details in *Henry
VI* (see p. 69), this episode again recalls what the Chinese
have called "the mandate of heaven," equally sanctioning
ruthless new dynasties, such as the Chin and the Manchu,
or new revolutionary states like that of the Communists
(whose authority in China was promptly recognized by
Britain on the same principle of effective supremacy as
that which supported the loyalty of the citizens of
Angiers). One might note that the medieval legal device
of trial by combat, and the "western" motif of the gun-
fight, equally depend on acceptance of a comparable
premise, which may be held to be either "providential"
or skeptical in conception, according to one's taste: either
way, the "best" man always wins.

However, as a kind of catalyst of the diplomatic ferment
before the gates of Angiers, the Bastard proposes that the
opposed kings teach the aloof citizens a lesson, by ravaging
their town before proceeding to a further mutual decima-
tion. Again the proposal is laden with Swiftian irony,
utterly unperceived by its crudely bellicose hearers. One
cannot but wonder that John's grasping spirit does not
recognize the ultimate fatuity of his appreciation of the
Bastard's malicious suggestion:

Now, by the sky that hangs above our heads,
I like it well. France, shall we knit our powers
And lay this Angiers even with the ground;
Then after fight who shall be king of it?

(II.i.397–400)

After it has been razed, why fight over its ruins? The
Bastard, by contrast, proves likely to have subtler purposes
in breaking the deadlock, since it turns out, to begin with,
that John's two enemies are thus disadvantaged by the
subsequent disposition of their two armies on facing sides
of the town:

> O prudent discipline! From north to south:
> Austria and France shoot in each other's mouth:
> I'll stir them to it. Come, away, away!
> (II.i.413–15)

Secondly, by shifting the onus of responsibility from the
headstrong monarchs, the Bastard forces the now directly
engaged but still prudent citizens to intervene, and to
achieve a compromise between the greedy but essentially
cowardly kings. Yet, even with a solution in sight, the
Bastard sustains his role of sarcastic chorus by ridiculing
the military rodomontade in which the citizens couch
their proposals for peace:

> Here's a stay
> That shakes the rotten carcass of old Death
> Out of his rags! Here's a large mouth, indeed,
> That spits forth death and mountains, rocks and seas,
> Talks as familiarly of roaring lions
> As maids at thirteen do of puppy-dogs! . . .
> Zounds! I was never so bethump'd with words
> Since I first call'd my brother's father dad.
> (II.i.455–60,466–7)

But while the Bastard is still engaged in ridiculing
middle-class affectation of courtly violence, Elinor is ad-
vising her son, John, to copy the selfish wisdom of the
burghers by accepting their compromise of an interdynas-
tic marriage, and then bribing the French king to abandon
Arthur's cause by giving "with our niece a dowry large
enough" (II.i.469). John follows her suggestion with a
gross indifference to all but the maintenance of his throne
in England, proposing as dowry the whole of the English
territories in France, barring only Angiers itself. After this

proposal, it is scarcely surprising that the Dauphin finds
the Lady Blanche to be possessed of a fascinating eye,
albeit one in which he chiefly notes his own complacent
reflection, as the Bastard caustically observes (II.i.504ff.).
In fact, the end of the act confirms the validity of the
Bastard's skepticism with regard to all human protestations
of virtue of any kind, and he concludes the scene with a
choric speech that confirms this impression:

> Mad world! mad kings! mad composition!
> John, to stop Arthur's title in the whole,
> Hath willingly departed with a part,
> And France, whose armour conscience buckled on,
> Whom zeal and charity brought to the field
> As God's own soldier, rounded in the ear
> With that same purpose-changer, that sly devil,
> That broker, that still breaks the pate of faith,
> That daily break-vow, he that wins of all,
> Of kings, of beggars, old men, young men, maids,
> Who having no external thing to lose
> But that word 'maid,' cheats the poor maid of that,
> That smooth-faced gentleman, tickling Commodity, . . .
> And why rail I on this Commodity?
> But for because he hath not woo'd me yet: . . .
> Since kings break faith upon commodity,
> Gain, be my lord, for I will worship thee.
> (II.i.561–73,587–8,597–9)

Once again the Bastard has emerged as the symbolic
pivot of the play. Yet, as an incidental character, he may
rationalize its action without his detached lucidity doing
damage to the historical plausibility of the behavior of any
figure as central to the plot of the play as Richard III was
in his. Richard both brilliantly manipulated historical
forces and abruptly fell victim to them, a paradox that is
here avoided by divorcing the performance of John from
the perceptions of the Bastard. Only as long as these two
characters remain in alliance will John be able to come
close to Richard's political mastery. John himself is an
opportunist without insight, and survives only so long as

he invites the support of the politically sophisticated, who would never allow themselves to be betrayed into his contemptible dilemmas.

In Act III, startlingly enough, we see just why the unstable John is nevertheless able to command the support of a character as perceptive as the Bastard. One reason certainly is that a cowardly cynic is a safer leader than a headstrong idealist. The act opens with a terrifying example of militant righteousness in the person of Constance, mother of the betrayed Prince Arthur. She is justified in her denunciations of the new treaty by the Bastard's preceding contemptuous analysis of Commodity; but while he coolly accepts it as the way of the world, she is incandescent with outraged virtue, as she admonishes Arthur:

> Fortune, O,
> She is corrupted, changed and won from thee;
> She adulterates hourly with thine uncle John,
> And with her golden hand hath pluck'd on France
> To tread down fair respect of sovereignty.
> (III.i.54–8)

After over a hundred lines of her almost uninterrupted denunciation of all and sundry, one begins to understand why one of John's concerns in concluding the marriage was to "satisfy" Constance, so "That we shall stop her exclamation" (II.i.558). However, just as Constance begins to become as wearisome to the audience as she is embarrassing to her late allies, her concern for abstract justice receives a powerful reinforcement in the person of the papal legate, Cardinal Pandulph. Thus political and religious sanctions are legitimately massed against John; but he is by now fully alert to the sole foundation of his authority, one that was necessarily clear to Shakespeare, as a subject of the usurping Protestant Tudors. The right to rule is frequently authorized by the power to rule. There would be a powerful approval in the Elizabethan audience's response to John's rejection of papal claims to authority in England:

What earthy name to interrogatories
Can task the free breath of a sacred king?
Thou canst not, cardinal, devise a name
So slight, unworthy and ridiculous,
To charge me to an answer, as the pope.
Tell him this tale; and from the mouth of England
Add thus much more, that no Italian priest
Shall tithe or toll in our dominions;
But as we, under heaven, are supreme head,
So under Him that great supremacy,
Where we do reign, we will alone uphold,
Without the assistance of a mortal hand.
(III.i.147–58)

This doctrine would, of course, be extremely palatable
to the Tudors, and more specifically to Queen Elizabeth,
Shakespeare's patron, in that the terms of reference could
readily be transposed to undercut the contemporary papal
attempts to subvert her authority through the powers of
King Philip II of Spain (as in the voyage of the Armada).
King Philip of France is cast in the comparable role of
the Pope's "strongman" in *King John;* but it is to Shakespeare's credit as a dramatist that he is no courtly time-
server, and neither falsely idealizes John's role (as did
some Tudor propagandists) nor caricatures the arguments
by means of which Pandulph wins the support of the
French king. The king is in some genuine distress at being
ordered to renew the battle with John on the very day of
the marriage that consummates their peace treaty. Pandulph's subtle and not wholly unconvincing argument for
loyalty to the highest ecclesiastical sanctions requires for
its success the emotional reinforcement of the Dauphin's
renewed enthusiasm for war against the English, which
now rises as conveniently as had his soon-cooled passion
for his English lady.

The Bastard's judgment of the Dauphin's amatory extravagance as that of "a vile lout" is now seen to be
plainly justified, and Blanche's desperate entreaties alone
give a touch of true tragedy to the scene, anticipating the

comparably divided loyalties of Juliet and Octavia. Pragmatist as she is, like almost all the English, Blanche cannot understand how metaphysical consistency can be valued more highly than men's lives. For her the easier alternative to renewed war is "the curse of Rome." No wonder that in such an atmosphere, with the renewal of battle, the Bastard's vivacity declines as his military prowess heightens. When he carries in the head of the Duke of Austria, whom he has slain in battle, he rightly senses the changed emotional climate:

Now, by my life, this day grows wondrous hot;
Some airy devil hovers in the sky
And pours down mischief.
         (III.ii.1–3)

Just how complex this "mischief" has now become appears in the tangle of conflicting values and loyalties in the two scenes that follow. In the first, John gives the Bastard orders to pillage the monasteries in England, which he sets out cheerfully to do—no doubt with the sympathy of the Elizabethan audiences, some of whom were certainly themselves still profiting from similar undertakings in the reign of King Henry VIII. But immediately afterwards, John plots with Hubert the death of the innocent Arthur, in terms that deliberately recall the murder of the Princes in the Tower, which was popularly held to be Richard III's most monstrous act. The audience is thus left with deeply divided loyalties, to which the sequel adds a surprising commentary. John had planned to dismantle the resources of the church and assassinate his innocent rival to the throne, yet his withdrawal from France is happily accomplished, and his enemies are left in defeated amazement at his prowess and good fortune. The naive Dauphin is particularly surprised by this blow to his self-complacency:

What he hath won, that hath he fortified:
So hot a speed with such advice disposed,
Such temperate order in so fierce a cause,

Doth want example: who hath read or heard
Of any kindred action like to this?
(III.iv.10–14)

The moral of this strategic triumph of John's lies precisely in the irrelevance to it of any moral considerations:
it shatters the conventional belief that violation of the
code of religious sanctions is necessarily followed by the
appropriate divine retribution, along the lines rigidly followed in the plot by Richard III. The Dauphin is far less
skeptical than the Bastard. Pandulph says to him "How
green you are and fresh in this old world!" (III.iv.145).
The reproach is occasioned by the Dauphin's abrupt swing
into nihilism as the result of John's success, a nihilism that
surpasses even that of the Bastard, and verges on the utter
despair and apathy of the declining Macbeth:

There's nothing in this world can make me joy:
Life is as tedious as a twice-told tale
Vexing the dull ear of a drowsy man;
And bitter shame hath spoil'd the sweet world's taste,
That it yields naught but shame and bitterness.
(III.iv.107–11)

In a world of cynical political maneuvers, an idealist such
as the Dauphin is as hopelessly disadvantaged as Romeo:
readily misled, self-deceiving, and prone to dislocating dis-
illusionment.

Nevertheless it might appear that, braced as the Dauphin
is by Pandulph's renewed arguments for pressing the war
against John, the events in Act IV work strongly for the
Dauphin and decisively against all John's hopes for further
success, as his moral obliquity finally begins to give rise
to disastrous political repercussions. The celebrated first
scene of the act, in which Hubert refuses to carry out
John's murderous designs on Arthur, intensifies our disgust
with so cruel a ruler; it is immediately followed by the
second crowning of John as king, an event which, as
Pembroke and Salisbury insist, serves rather to question
than to confirm the validity of his first coronation. At

best it serves only "to gild refined gold, to paint the lily" (IV.ii.11); at worst:

> When workmen strive to do better than well,
> They do confound their skill in covetousness;
> And oftentimes excusing of a fault
> Doth make the fault the worse by the excuse,
> As patches set upon a little breach
> Discredit more in hiding of the fault
> Than did the fault before it was so patch'd.
>   (IV.ii.28–34)

John thus finally emerges in the eyes of his subjects not only as morally suspect, but as politically incompetent in direct correlation with this deficiency, just as the Dauphin had originally hoped. Indeed, as soon as John announces Arthur's supposed death, his nobles' suspicions of the king's integrity become certainties:

> Indeed we heard how near his death he was
> Before the child himself felt he was sick:
> This must be answer'd either here or hence.
>   (IV.ii.87–9)

The rest of the act is devoted to a systematic account of John's crumbling hold on his kingdom, affected by prophecies and rumors among the common people, and to the open revolt of the aristocracy, despite the double reversal of expectation involved in Arthur's death. Yet, once again the Bastard's perspective provides a clue to the dramatist's own vision. Faulconbridge refuses to find John guilty on circumstantial evidence and, although he is deeply disturbed at the mere possibility of Hubert's guilt, he refuses to sanction the savage lynch law invoked by Pembroke, who wants to "cut him to pieces" (IV.iii.93). Yet, even while he strenuously orders them to "Keep the peace," the Bastard no longer moves through the deepening morass of human misfortunes and duplicities with the confident ease of the cynic. He is too profoundly touched by the death of the child to remain his old insouciant self:

> Go, bear him in thine arms.
> I am amazed, methinks, and lose my way
> Among the thorns and dangers of this world.
> How easy dost thou take all England up!
> From forth this morsel of dead royalty,
> The life, the right, and truth of all this realm
> Is fled to heaven. . . .
>
> (IV.iii.139–45)

It is crucial to note that this last speech of the Bastard in Act IV concludes, correctly, by not finding John guilty in practice of Arthur's death, however much he may have solicited it. While, with her death, John has lost the guileful counsel of his mother as well as the loyalty of many of his supporters, he has not been adequately convicted of a criminal act, and the symbolic loyalty of the Bastard suggests that the balance of national opinion has not even now swung decisively against John. Ironically, while the death of Arthur immediately alienates some of John's more naive supporters, such as Pembroke and Salisbury, it also lends a new seriousness to men like the Bastard, who have hitherto appeared to be mere adventurers. The account of their future conduct is to reflect a discrimination in the author's political values that is markedly superior in practical terms to the apparently worthier principles of men like Pembroke, Salisbury, and the Dauphin.

Act V presents us with a weird counterpoint of advances and reversals of fortune in which the vigorous if somewhat skeptical patriotism of the Bastard alone provides an element of consistency. John makes his peace with Rome in politic fashion, patching up the religious quarrel that had lent color to the new French invasion of England's territories. But the Bastard warns the king against believing in Pandulph's capacity to live up to his promise that, with John's restored loyalty to the Church:

> My tongue shall hush again the storm of war
> And make fair weather in your blustering land.
>
> (V.i.20–1)

To the Bastard the promise is a pathetic resource on which to rely for one's authority. He sneers at this "inglorious league," asking:

> Shall we, upon the footing of our land,
> Send fair-play orders and make compromise,
> Insinuation, parley and base truce
> To arms invasive?
> (V.i.66–9)

The matter is now too serious for the Bastard to take a stand on the narrower issue of John's moral failures as an individual; and as John sinks into guilt-ridden lethargy, and thence into a fever that is the prelude to his supposed death by poison, the Bastard relentlessly strives to create at least that appearance of authority that the Crown of England requires (whatever the private character of its wearer), if England itself is to survive:

> . . . wherefore do you droop? why look you sad?
> Be great in act, as you have been in thought;
> Let not the world see fear and sad distrust
> Govern the motion of a kingly eye:
> Be stirring as the time; be fire with fire;
> Threaten the threatener and outface the brow
> Of bragging horror: so shall inferior eyes,
> That borrow their behaviours from the great,
> Grow great by your example and put on
> The dauntless spirit of resolution.
> (V.i.44–53)

There is a kind of ruthless practical psychology here which rationalizes the hearty behavior of the declining Richard III on the battlefield before his defeat and death at the hands of Richmond. At certain moments the King of England necessarily acts only as King and not at all as a private man—however guilty he may be. In some senses, the King is thus two persons: "This distinction between the rights and obligations of the crown, and the person of the monarch, is more central to the development of the English constitution than representative institutions, which came much later, and which indeed it made possible. The crown was the fountain of justice; but the king himself was subject to law and custom" as Paul Johnson writes.[1] Shakespeare shows the Bastard Faulconbridge seeking to preserve England's independence of France on the basis of this duality. On the one hand, the Bastard accurately reflects the terms of the play in reluctantly giving John the benefit of the doubt in the matter of the death of Arthur; but in his capacity as servant of the King of England, his heroic requirements of the shifty John would seem ludicrous, were it not for the sense of the transcendence of the man by his office.

Faulconbridge's patriotic attitude carries conviction in exact proportion as the English nobles in revolt fail to convince themselves that their hatred of John provides an adequate basis for a political action so ominous as desertion to the enemy. Salisbury is defeated even before he begins the battle against his compatriots:

> And is't not pity, O my grieved friends,
> That we, the sons and children of this isle,
> Were born to see so sad an hour as this:
> Wherein we step after a stranger march
> Upon her gentle bosom, and fill up
> Her enemies' ranks,—I must withdraw and weep
> Upon the spot of this enforced cause,—
> To grace the gentry of a land remote,
> And follow unacquainted colours here?
> (V.ii.24-32)

One begins to see the peculiar symbolic truth both of the Bastard's hearty indifference at the start of the play to questions of private fortune and dignity, and of his decision to follow the larger, less personal goal of service to the Crown—to which he is unflinchingly loyal, despite his ironies at the expense of its wearer. It is significant that,

[1] *New Statesman* (London, November 1, 1963), reviewing *The Government of Mediaeval England* by H. G. Richardson. See also E. H. Kantorowicz, *The King's Two Bodies* (Princeton, 1957).

in his capacity as the spirit of dynamic political action, his analysis of the French contempt for Pandulph's renewed peacemaking efforts proves valid, and that he is thereupon able to speak as the voice of a resolved and prepared England. He pours scorn on the shallow judgment of the rebellious English nobles, who are thereafter inevitably the victims of any suggestion that further diminishes their self-confidence, as when the dying French Count Melun warns them:

> Fly, noble English, you are bought and sold;
> Unthread the rude eye of rebellion
> And welcome home again discarded faith.
> Seek out King John and fall before his feet;
> For if the French be lords of this loud day,
> He means to recompense the pains you take
> By cutting off your heads: thus hath he sworn
> And I with him, and many more with me
> Upon the altar at St. Edmundsbury.
>   (V.iv.10–18)

It scarcely matters whether the warning is true or not, for the traitors are already unnerved: Salisbury exclaims "I did not think the king so stored with friends" (V.iv.1) and bitterly recognizes that "in spite of spite" the English army is sustained alone by "That misbegotten devil, Faulconbridge," even after John has left the field "sore sick." Mere nerve, and a clear political sense thus carry Faulconbridge through, while a wavering moral conviction, at odds with their political instincts, saps the loyalty of the Dauphin's English allies. It must be noted meanwhile that, unlike *Richard III*, the play offers no evidence for a simple providential judgment by God, either against the "immoral" John, or for him. Both the English and the French are shown to suffer equally from "acts of God," through the agency of the onslaught of the elements. The French fleet is cast away on the Goodwin Sands, and Faulconbridge loses half his army in "these Lincoln Washes," where it has been caught by the tide. What turns the balance in favor of England is thus simply the steady political and military energy of the Bastard, which is rooted in a sense of true English identity. However, once the potency of this native English resentment of foreign invasion becomes clear to the French, their inclination to make peace is reinforced by those plausible arguments for peace on the part of Cardinal Pandulph that were originally set afoot by John's cunning surrender to Rome. The effective use of the weight of conventional legal authority combines with merely crafty political manipulation to establish the invincibility of the English crown—whatever the private failings and mongrel origins of the individuals involved in its defense. The Bastard concludes the play with a ringing reassertion of that national solidarity that has carried the day:

> O, let us pay the time but needful woe,
> Since it hath been beforehand with our griefs.
> This England never did, nor never shall,
> Lie at the proud feet of a conqueror,
> But when it first did help to wound itself.
> Now these her princes are come home again,
> Come the three corners of the world in arms,
> And we shall shock them. Nought shall make us rue,
> If England to itself do rest but true.
>   (V.vii.110–18)

 *III*

THE SECOND TETRALOGY

I

🕐 *Richard II*

       Richard II may be related to *King John* by its deliberate choice of yet another reign whose erratic character invited an ambiguous response in Elizabethan Englishmen, like the "saintly" incompetence of Henry VI's administration, or the feebly crafty yet anti-papal orientation of John's. The play also achieves a more exciting recombination of the political resources previously shared between John and the Bastard, which are now shown to be not in alliance but in opposition. John's cunning and the Bastard's pragmatic political sense fall to the lot of Bolingbroke, while the verve and rhetorical color of the Bastard combine, in Richard, with a certain rashness and moral casualness that had been shared by both John and his supporter. The result is a striking increase in dramatic tension; whatever the dates of composition of the two plays, *Richard II* is superior both in its language and in its political sophistication, not to mention its subtlety of characterization. Indeed, the hypnotic rhetoric of Richard and the progression of his personality and his career have encouraged critics to think of the play as essentially the individual tragedy of his fall from eminence. This is a distortion, for from the first scene to the last the real issues are never based on Richard's exclusive concerns, but bear directly on his role in the body politic. In fact, the commentators' over-concern with the idea that tragedy is based on the convention of a flawed hero, coupled with their rather casual attitude to the com-

plex political tensions throughout the play, have often resulted in their misreading not only the action of the play,
but equally the character of Richard himself.

The opening scene, for example, establishes a masterly
counterpoint between the bravura of formal political debate in the medieval style and the treacherous, indeed
murderous events and instincts that really govern these
highly rhetorical performances. In line with that preservation of the distinction between the absolute integrity of
the Crown and the personal fallibility of its human component that we first noted in *King John*, Bolingbroke's
challenging of Mowbray appears to be merely an example
of one local lapse in the administration of government resources, thereby entirely avoiding the formal involvement
of the king's reputation in such matters. Yet at the heart of
Bolingbroke's challenge of Mowbray lies a veiled threat
to Richard himself, as the implied initiator of Mowbray's
actions, and particularly of the assassination in Calais of
Thomas of Woodstock, Duke of Gloucester, who was the
uncle of both Richard and Bolingbroke. Richard is thus
in certain senses both judge and defendant in Bolingbroke's somewhat specious case against Mowbray, as Gaunt
unhappily admits to Gloucester's widow at the start of the
next scene:

> Alas, the part I had in Woodstock's blood
> Doth more solicit me than your exclaims,
> To stir against the butchers of his life!
> But since correction lieth in those hands
> Which made the fault that we cannot correct,
> Put we our quarrel to the will of heaven.
>
> (I.ii.1–6)

The implicit ambiguity of Richard's position in the opening scene may thus seem to invite an unsympathetic response toward him on our part, and indeed, at one level
of interpretation, Bolingbroke plausibly appears to be the
champion of family honor and loyalty.

Unfortunately, at another level he is chiefly concerned
with undermining Richard's authority and even the very

basis of his survival. In this, Bolingbroke's course proves analogous to (but more discreet than) that goal of deposing and even assassinating Richard, which had historically forced the king to arrange in self-defense for his uncle's assassination. As a further complication it turns out, later in the play (IV.i.80–2), that Mowbray is in fact to be held as innocent of the murder of Gloucester as he earlier protested, even while recognizing that there were indeed valid grounds for such an act:

> For Gloucester's death,
> I slew him not; but to my own disgrace
> Neglected my sworn duty in that case.
> (I.i.132–4)

This statement may be readily understood to mean that loyalty to Richard as King of England requires all his subjects to protect him from the mischievous plots of such envious relatives as Gloucester. In one way, therefore, we may with justice begin to wonder whether Richard's situation is not closer to that of the doomed young Edward V in *Richard III* than to that of the would-be assassin who wears the crown in *King John*. Richard's father was a hero—the Black Prince, heir to Edward III; but since he had died before Edward, Richard had succeeded his grandfather on the throne at the tender age of ten, with consequent strain on his relationship with his gifted and experienced uncles. Their resentment, both veiled and open, surrounds Richard like a sinister miasma from the very opening of the play, often breaking out into savage vituperation, as in Gaunt's dying speeches:

> O, had thy grandsire with a prophet's eye
> Seen how his son's son should destroy his sons,
> From forth thy reach he would have laid thy shame,
> Deposing thee before thou wert possess'd,
> Which art possess'd now to depose thyself.
> (II.i.104–8)

There needs only a little extension of this sentiment to justify such acts as those meditated by Gloucester; it is hard not to see in Bolingbroke's challenge to Mowbray the calculated jostling of the throne by a rival cousin who hoped to shake down the fortunate heir to the crown.

In fact, in the context of these intense family pressures, it is surprising that Richard manages to maintain his poise as well as he does in the opening scenes. If anything, Richard's self-possession reflects the dangerous assumption that he enjoys unlimited freedom of action. Despite an unmistakable intellectual superiority to those around him, Richard fails to concern himself sufficiently with the political currents that are swirling just beneath the surface. He stops to reason and argue instead of taking a decisive role, as Bolingbroke so arrogantly does in the analogous situation that arises, when he begins to assume command of England (IV.i.86ff.). Richard continually reflects that almost casual freedom of expression and action of the Bastard Faulconbridge that had remained incidental to the central pattern of most of *King John*, but which in *Richard II* becomes a fatal complication in the needful impersonality of Richard's administration.

Richard's fault thus does not lie in any simple defect of private personality. He is certainly not as deeply vicious as Gaunt would have us believe in his famous deathbed denunciation (II.i.93ff.), for Richard's return from Ireland to his kingdom is marked by almost as intense a statement of devotion to his native land (III.ii.4ff.) as that of Gaunt in his famous celebration of "This blessed plot, this earth, this realm, this England" in Act II, Scene i. Nor is Richard incapable of the most graceful gestures of kingly mercy, as when he spares Bolingbroke the full term of his exile, remitting four of his ten years of exile in consideration of the grief of Bolingbroke's father, Gaunt. Nor will it do to censure the judgment passed by Richard on the intended combatants at the tournament, since it is clearly established that this is in no sense the result of a spontaneous gesture on the part of the king. Richard orders them to hear, not his personal verdict, but "what with our council we have done" (I.iii.124); and, in the case of Mowbray at least, the council's decision is one "Which I with some unwillingness pronounce" (I.iii.149), so that there seems some justification for Richard's resentment at Gaunt's response to his son's reduced sentence:

Thy son is banished upon good advice,
Whereto thy tongue a party-verdict gave:
Why at our justice seem'st thou then to lour?

(I.iii.233-5)

Altogether there seems, if anything, too great a spirit of conciliation and spontaneous good nature in Richard's actions during these early scenes, rather than any moral weakness or viciousness.

The one point on which he has been censured on plausible grounds is the *manner* of his conduct, which inflates the actual status of an issue to the disadvantage of a swift and decisive settlement. Richard mistakes the visibility of an action for the effective accomplishment of its aim. In *King John* we have already seen how effective government offsets the apparently fatal consequences of a poor public showing. In *Richard II*, on the other hand, we see that neither legitimate authority nor a dashing public figure is enough to sustain an effective administration. Bolingbroke lacks Richard's intellectual verve and imaginative potential, as we can see in his dreary response to the consolations offered for his exile:

O, who can hold a fire in his hand
By thinking on the frosty Caucasus?
Or cloy the hungry edge of appetite
By bare imagination of a feast?

(I.iii.294-7)

On the other hand, Bolingbroke has the tightest grasp on political realities and can therefore turn every occasion to personal advantage, as Richard quickwittedly, but altogether too contemptuously recognizes. At Bolingbroke's departure, Richard tells how he has

Observed his courtship to the common people;
How he did seem to dive into their hearts
With humble and familiar courtesy,
What reverence he did throw away on slaves,
Wooing poor craftsmen with the craft of smiles
And patient underbearing of his fortune.

(I.iv.24-9)

The fact is that Richard would have been well-advised from the start to redirect his own freeswinging personality toward a similar exploitation of his political advantages. While Richard despises such narrow considerations, his casualness results in hasty administrative judgments, as when he sells off his resources of taxation for ready cash (I.iv.42ff.). In such matters, he is often guilty of flippancy and even of bad taste, as in his jibe at the news of Gaunt's decline:

Now put it, God, in the physician's mind
To help him to his grave immediately!
The lining of his coffers shall make coats
To deck our soldiers for these Irish Wars.

(I.iv.59-62)

Richard's primary tactical mistake in the play is to translate this unfortunate inspiration into action, under the spur of the dying Gaunt's own vehement wish to dispossess Richard himself of his birthright. York's feeble attempt to soften the king's resentment by arguing that Gaunt loves him as dearly as does Bolingbroke sets off in the king's alert mind an exactly antithetical reaction to the one that was intended:

Right, you say true: as Hereford's love, so his;
As theirs, so mine; and all be as it is.

(II.i.145-6)

Under the emotional tension of the recurring threats of deposition arising out of the hatred of his relatives, the king as usual acts spontaneously and without weighing the political consequences. He too readily shrugs off York's laborious exposition of them:

Take Hereford's rights away, and take from Time
His charters and his customary rights;
Let not tomorrow then ensue to-day;
Be not thyself; for how art thou a king
But by fair sequence and succession?
                    (II.i.195–9)

Richard is continually being betrayed by the family rivalries into courses of conduct such as this one which invites
further calculated challenges to his authority. The murder
of Gloucester, plausibly ascribed to Richard (though this
is never proved in the play), would thus be no random
act of viciousness, but a desperate gesture of self-defense
on Richard's part. In its turn, the murder lent color to the
diffusion of Gloucester's rebellious mood throughout the
entire family.

While it must be acknowledged that Richard's seizure
of the dead Gaunt's lands constitutes a dangerous precedent and reflects Richard's poor political tact, we must also
recognize that it cannot be the original pretext for Bolingbroke's return in the play, even though he is shown characteristically to twist it to this advantage, upon landing.
For the very scene in which Richard announces his seizure
of his uncle's estate, and is thereupon admonished by York,
concludes with Northumberland's revelation that Bolingbroke has already left the Continent, to which he had been
exiled, and is thus launched on his armed return to England well before Richard's politically unfortunate act.
Bolingbroke has a group of distinguished followers, listed
by Northumberland, and:

All these well furnish'd by the Duke of Bretagne
With eight tall ships, three thousand men of war,
Are making hither with all due expedience
And shortly mean to touch our northern shore:
Perhaps they had ere this but that they stay
The first departing of the king for Ireland.
                    (II.i.285–90)

Thus, if Richard is fighting—often brutally but with
some traces of dignity and much immediate justification—

to preserve his legitimate authority, Bolingbroke from the start sustains Gloucester's anarchistic initiative, and ultimately becomes a traitor, greedy for power, even though he is masterful in finding plausible color for all his actions. He unquestionably incarnates all that coarse but efficient opportunism that Richard's finer character instinctively fails to cultivate, and into which he lapses awkwardly, and only when under acute pressure. The tragedy of Richard is not what nineteenth-century critical fashion would have him share with Hamlet—the failure of the merely "poetic" temperament to cope with realities. It is much rather the disaster that results when opportunism is not curbed by superior cunning, achieved at perhaps an even higher cost to private moral worth than Richard resentfully pays.

The famous garden scene establishes the universal necessity for the sort of brutal rigor that the high-minded ruler must cultivate in order to sustain his other, more civilized resources. The Gardener symbolically maintains a ruthless order in his little Commonwealth, telling his fellow servants:

> Go thou, and like an executioner,
> Cut off the heads of too fast growing sprays
> That look too lofty in our commonwealth:
> All must be even in our government.
> You thus employ'd, I will go root away
> The noisome weeds, which without profit suck
> The soil's fertility from wholesome flowers.
>
> (III.iv.33–9)

The discussion then progresses naturally to the king's failure to maintain a similarly firm discipline in his larger territory:

> O, what a pity is it
> That he had not so trimm'd and dress'd his land
> As we this garden! We at time of year
> Do wound the bark, the skin of our fruit-trees,
> Lest, being over-proud in sap and blood,
> With too much riches it confound itself:

Had he done so to great and growing men,
They might have lived to bear and he to taste
Their fruits of duty.
　　(III.iv.55–63)

The reproach is thus that Richard is too lenient and generous. The Gardener is clearly concerned primarily with
expressing approval of Bolingbroke's execution of Bushy
and Green; but the generalizations might apply equally to
anyone (including Bolingbroke himself) who had raised
his head too high for the king's (and the kingdom's)
peace.

In fact, Bolingbroke's severity against Richard's supporters is shown to be little more than a caricature of
justice: his accusations are vague, for the most part: "You
have misled a prince" (III.i.8), or fatuous, as when he
accuses them of having "Made a divorce betwixt his queen
and him" (III.i.12)—a fault, incidentally, of which he may
be later accused far more legitimately himself (V.i.51–102).
Bolingbroke's most precisely urged charges against
Richard's men are also the most private and local:

　　. . . you have fed upon my signories,
Dispark'd my parks and fell'd my forest woods,
From my own windows torn my household coat,
Razed out my imprese, leaving me no sign,
Save men's opinions and my living blood
To show the world I am a gentleman.
　　　　(III.i.22–7)

The charges are plausible enough, but if Richard is initially tainted in Act I for judging a case (and compara-
tively how mildly!) to which he was himself a party, then
Bolingbroke is here far more culpable for usurping a
judicial role to which he has no title whatsoever, as well
as being overtly compromised in the case, in which he
appears as plaintiff, prosecutor, and judge.

Bolingbroke is basically a ruthless manipulator of political forces, indifferent to any larger issues than those

dictated by expediency, as he is later made to confess on his deathbed to his son:

> God knows, my son,
> By what by-paths and indirect and crook'd ways
> I met this crown; and I myself know well
> How troublesome it sat upon my head.
> (*2HIV*, IV.v.184–7)

In many ways Richard is the exact opposite of this antagonist: fluent and generous, where Bolingbroke is constrained and surly; ideologically sophisticated, rather than grimly pragmatic; loving free debate and discussion, whereas Bolingbroke is either unctuous or blunt and ruthless. Above all, Richard is a man who is more deeply aware of the possibilities of human volition: he perpetually gives the impression of a man who chooses his course of conduct consciously, however metaphysically or abruptly he may seem to do so. By contrast, Bolingbroke moves almost without volition through the currents of political life, deciding his conduct instead by instinctive reflexes, as in his clever tactics during the deposition scene.

The limitations of Richard's temperament are best illustrated by his earlier behavior, on his return to his kingdom from Ireland, when his sense of his own nominal authority is sharply juxtaposed with the consequences of overmuch dependence on the consistency of attitude of those to whom he has too confidently trusted the kingdom during his absence abroad (perhaps his worst strategic error). Richard's notorious overconfidence at the start of this scene is not quite as grotesquely unrealistic as it might appear. It is true that he has an almost ecstatic conviction of his own power:

> This earth shall have a feeling and these stones
> Prove armed soldiers, ere her native king
> Shall falter under foul rebellion's arms.
> (III.ii.24–6)

and it is also true that Aumerle reinforces the bishop's admonition to Richard not to depend only on God's will, but also to use "the means that heaven yields." It has been a theme of reproach to Richard that he replies to his "discomfortable cousin" by reiterating his faith in the principle that "heaven still guards the right." In the context of this argument, it now appears somewhat ironic that, in the proposal for a tournament with which the play begins, Richard was not content to leave the matter to such arbitration. However, it remains doubtful whether Richard's confidence on his return to England is even then considered fairly to be based on trust in providence alone. At this point he still quite reasonably expects more than adequate military resources to be supplied by Salisbury and York, whose vacillations and incompetence defy any anticipation. One would be almost as unfair to blame Richard for his early optimism while awaiting the arrival of these armies, as for being cast down and pale thereafter, when he learns that they do not exist:

> But now the blood of twenty thousand men
> Did triumph in my face, and they are fled;
> And, till to so much blood thither come again,
> Have I not reason to look pale and dead?
>
> (III.ii.76–9)

It is scarcely surprising that his thoughts now turn to "sad stories of the death of kings"; he knows his enemy too well to hope for such mercy as he himself had accorded Bolingbroke in reducing his exile. Bolingbroke's reflexes will be, as always, toward ruthlessness; his mercies are merely calculated.

Richard's sole remaining weapon lies in his maturing psychological subtlety, as we can see this reflected in his formal intellectual and rhetorical power. Wherever possible, he uses such resources boldly and with increasing political impact as he accumulates bitter first-hand experience. His public posture after his capture at Flint is only momentarily imposing, but by the time of the famous deposition scene his impact, both political and emotional, on the court and on the play's audience matches Bolingbroke's more evenly than ever before. This is prefigured in the Bishop of Carlisle's powerful attack on Bolingbroke's brusque announcement, "In God's name, I'll ascend the regal throne" (IV.i.113).

The naked power that alone vindicates Bolingbroke's proceedings continually conflicts with the human intensity and increasingly bitter self-awareness of Richard. He even manages to resist the relentless pressure of Northumberland to recite his "grievous crimes." Bolingbroke backs down when he begins to realize the potency of Richard's rhetoric in his resistance to humiliation:

> Must I do so? and must I ravel out
> My weaved-up folly? Gentle Northumberland,
> If thy offences were upon record,
> Would it not shame thee in so fair a troop
> To read a lecture of them? If thou wouldst,
> There shouldst thou find a heinous article,
> Containing the deposing of a king
> And cracking the strong warrant of an oath
> Mark'd with a blot, damn'd in the book of heaven: . . .
> Mine eyes are full of tears, I cannot see:
> And yet salt water blinds them not so much
> But they can see a sort of traitors here.
> Nay, if I turn mine eyes upon myself,
> I find myself a traitor with the rest;
> For I have given here my soul's consent
> To undeck the pompous body of a king;
> Made glory base and sovereignty a slave,
> Proud majesty a subject, state a peasant.
>   (IV.i.228–36, 244–52)

The stature of Richard here begins to approach the heroic, as his self-realization and indignation fuse his personality into a coherent whole, in which mind and action become one. Shakespeare is too wise, of course, to present us with the spectacle of an alert young man matured instantly and irrevocably into a powerful and commanding personality. Not only has Richard by now completely lost the physical initiative to Bolingbroke, just at the moment

when he attains the moral authority to which he aspired
in the opening scenes, but Richard still favors discursive
debate at the expense of the immediate issue. He has attained to a clear sense of the conceptual order of which
the English crown has traditionally been the keystone,
only to digress speculatively on more subjective medita-
tions along tangents in which Bolingbroke is only too
happy to encourage him:

> *Bolingbroke:* The shadow of your sorrow hath destroy'd
> The shadow of your face.
> *King Richard:*   Say that again.
> The shadow of my sorrows! ha! let's see:
> 'Tis very true, . . .
> (IV.i.292–5)

Thus it is Richard's intellectual vivacity that deflects him
from his last opportunity to translate his now highly tuned
awareness of the philosophy of politics into direct action.
Only in his last moments will Richard finally achieve a
tigerish physical potency of the kind that earlier would
have been able to render ineffectual all of Bolingbroke's
tough, insinuating strokes.

Nevertheless, Richard unmistakably commands the last
scenes, just as Gaunt seems to dominate the opening ones.
When the grimly phlegmatic Northumberland separates
Richard abruptly from his queen, the deposed king
launches into a precise political forecast of his enemy's
fate, fully vindicated by the action of the first part of
Henry IV:

> Northumberland, thou ladder wherewithal
> The mounting Bolingbroke ascends my throne,
> The time shall not be many hours of age
> More than it is ere foul sin gathering head
> Shall break into corruption: thou shalt think,
> Though he divide the realm and give thee half,
> It is too little, helping him to all;
> And he shall think that thou, which know'st the way
> To plant unrightful kings, wilt know again,
> Being ne'er so little urged, another way

To pluck him headlong from the usurped throne.
The love of wicked men converts to fear;
That fear to hate, and hate turns one or both
To worthy danger and deserved death.
(V.i.55–68)

One has only to compare the authoritative tones of this
analysis with Richard's superficial plausibility in the opening scenes, to recognize how much he has matured. He no
longer commands respect by his status, which is now
negligible, but by his innate resources of personality.
While he continues to be publicly humiliated, he carries
this off with a dignity superior to the best he can muster
at his deposition, as even the turncoat York ruefully admits. After sketching Bolingbroke's triumph, he describes
Richard memorably:

But dust was thrown upon his sacred head;
Which with such gentle sorrow he shook off,
His face still combating with tears and smiles,
The badges of his grief and patience,
That had not God, for some strong purpose, steel'd
The hearts of men, they must perforce have melted
And barbarism itself have pitied him.
(V.ii.30–6)

The new order of Bolingbroke is rightly characterized
in York's account as one that is enforced by hard hearts
and barbarism. York himself does not see the irony of his
making new oaths of eternal loyalty to a new king so soon
after betraying the old one, nor does he fully recognize
the new emotional climate that civil strife has induced. In
this new order there will be less inclination for fathers to
seek, as did Gaunt, their sons' well-being. Not only does
York himself hound his son mercilessly for political reasons, but Bolingbroke's own son apparently revolts against
loyalty to so disloyal a man as his father:

Can no man tell me of my unthrifty son?
'Tis full three months since I did see him last:
If any plague hang over us, 'tis he.

I would to God, my lords, he might be found:
Inquire at London, 'mongst the taverns there,
For there, they say, he daily doth frequent,
With unrestrained loose companions, . . .
                                (V.iii.1–7)

The slack structure of this degenerate new society can
never hope to recover the finer temper that had characterized Richard's court, for all its strains and tensions. Richard
aspired to reason and to gallant generosity, even if he did
stoop to forced taxation and to revenge for injuries offered
or sustained. And while in all other ways Henry's kingdom
is to be worse than Richard's, Henry himself is no more
innocent of the instincts of the assassin than was Richard,
and far more culpable in practice, since he invites Richard's
murder, not so much in response to sustained threats of his
own assassination, such as had motivated Richard against
Gloucester, as to protect his stolen kingdom against even
the possibility of its restoration to the rightful ruler by
such figures as York's son Aumerle.

It is ironic that under the new king the bravest acts
are those that are associated with the deposed king.
Richard's last scene is the best evidence of that evolution
of his personality from a facile mustering of kingly dignity, perpetually at odds with youthful optimism and spontaneity, to a new, bitterly wise, and ruthless maturity.
This last scene is marked by an extraordinary fusion of resigned self-knowledge with physical resolution, a fusion
that is completely incompatible with the view of Richard
as an oversensitive poet, incapable of action. Richard's long
soliloquy is a more complete recognition of himself than
Shakespeare allows many of his political heroes:

> Music do I hear?
> Ha, ha! keep time: how sour sweet music is,
> When time is broke and no proportion kept!
> So is it in the music of men's lives.
> And here have I the daintiness of ear
> To check time broke in a disorder'd string;
> But for the concord of my state and time

Had not an ear to hear my true time broke.
I wasted time, and now doth time waste me; . . .

(V.v.41–9)

There is no longer any discrepancy between Richard's refined awareness and a firm grasp of effective reality. Not only does he instantly perceive the plot to poison him, but he reacts with extraordinary physical promptness to the assault by Exton and his servants. In Holinshed, Richard kills four of his nine assailants; in Shakespeare, only two, out of a presumably smaller number required for satisfactory staging. Either way we are presented with a figure who is no longer tragic but epic. Whatever the character of the historical Richard (and he was apparently at least as complex and impressive as Shakespeare makes him), there is no doubt that the dramatist follows Holinshed in wishing Richard's last moments to be an heroic apotheosis, a vindication of that archetypal authority that he had far too casually lost to Henry.

This is a tragedy for all concerned—for Richard, for England, *and* for Henry. Exton has barely epitomized Richard's final state of mind: "As full of valour as of royal blood" (V.v.114), before we are confronted with Henry's uneasy announcement of the difficulties his own example has invited:

Kind uncle York, the latest news we hear
Is that the rebels have consumed with fire
Our town of Cicester in Gloucestershire;
But whether they be ta'en or slain we hear not.

(V.vi.1–4)

These, the first of a long series of rebels, prove to have been defeated. Yet the play ends on Henry's attempt to shrug off any responsibility for Exton's murder of Richard, in a speech that closely echoes that of King John to Hubert, the supposed murderer of Prince Arthur:

They love not poison that do poison need,
Nor do I thee: though I did wish him dead,

I hate the murderer, love him murdered.
The guilt of conscience take thou for thy labour.

(V.vi.38–41)

Yet not so long before, according to Exton, Henry had said: "Have I no friend will rid me of this living fear?" (V.iv.2). Nor do we have Exton's word alone: Shakespeare is careful to corroborate the fact that Henry spoke the words twice, by providing the testimony of the servant to whom Exton is speaking. Henry's guilt is thus explicit in a way that Shakespeare has previously taken pains to ensure was not the case with Richard's involvement in the death of Gloucester.

One can only take consolation from the repercussions of Henry's dawning sense of his own guilt, which encourages a new element of mercifulness toward those who are more loyal than he was: Aumerle and Carlisle, Richard's best allies. Since they are "traitors" to the new king, policy might well argue for their deaths; but with the attainment of his ends there appear hints of new potentialities in Henry—the office begins to impose its own higher discipline on the man. However, the dignified rhetoric of the High Middle Ages, which made the first scenes of the play so stately, has been permanently invalidated by the disintegration of the medieval sense of hierarchy on which it depended—a sense of cosmic order that the Elizabethans recalled, with understandable nostalgia. For that metaphysical sanction of authority on which Richard II confidently depended, and which Henry VI somewhat skeptically solicited, Shakespeare's presentation of the reign of the first Lancastrian king substitutes the success of unequivocal power politics of the modern, pragmatic kind. Unfortunately, these politics justify not only the subversion of Richard II's immature and archaic rule, but also the subsequent destruction of the last Lancastrian, Henry VI, by a revitalized Yorkist party—and the ultimate extinction of these Yorkists in turn, by the Tudors. *Richard II* is thus intended to present a largely historical account of the political decline from the primal innocence of the ideal medieval society to a Machiavellian pragmatism in the modern vein. Shakespeare systematically identifies in Bolingbroke that new type of amoral personality to whom success and title will necessarily go in the modern political life that has been cut off from medieval cosmic values. He devotes the rest of his political plays to the investigation of whether such a personality, and the environment it creates, are in any way compatible with the practice of the archaic virtues and the Christian ideal.

2

Henry IV

Part One

SHAKESPEARE usually identifies respect for the Crown as the lynch-pin of society—even when its powers are cavalierly misdirected by such a figure as Richard II—but nothing stresses this point much more than the sad spectacle of the kingdom of England as it appears under Bolingbroke, now King Henry IV. He is king by might rather than right for, even with Richard dead, there were closer direct heirs than the Lancastrian branch of the Plantagenets led by Henry. Henry shows from the opening lines of *Henry IV* that he is master of that tactical skill whose lack was the major factor in Richard's initial loss of control. Henry's opening declamation is a masterpiece of calculation in the interests of preserving his all too precarious authority. Henry has the sense to see that, if he is to be identified adequately with the Crown, he must continually maintain the initiative, so that there is never time to raise the question of the legality of his succession. His proposal of a Crusade against the Moslems in the Holy Land is a stroke of political genius: the war will assert his authority, distract the more bellicose elements in English society, and suggest a proper piety in one who otherwise might be said to have stolen the Crown (alternatively, it might be held to be a fitting penance for a necessary but regrettable act).

There is, however, a further level of irony, for it soon becomes clear not only that the Crusade that Henry proposes has been rather promptly invalidated by the bad news of the Welsh rebellion that Westmoreland is forced to announce, but also that Henry from the start has scarcely expected to mount the expedition he so piously proposed. He therefore expresses no real surprise or distress at the breaking of his plans, saying only:

> It seems then that the tidings of this broil
> Brake off our business for the Holy Land.
> (I.i.47–8)

In fact, it may even appear that Westmoreland is being manipulated as a herald of evil tidings, for he is now led on to reveal other gloomy news, from Scotland. In this disturbing atmosphere, Henry is able to stage a further reassuring announcement: the happy outcome of the Scottish campaign, which he presents personally in order to suggest his own authoritative intelligence about English affairs. This efficiency further appears in his order to have Hotspur return to London in order to explain his misconduct in withholding his prisoners from the king.

However, the impression of competent authority that the king in this manner plausibly sustains is not borne out by the facts with which he has to cope. Not only does he have to meet invasions from the west and the north, which involve his own shaky succession, but his lieutenants, such as Mortimer and Hotspur, are either incompetent or unpredictable. And more serious still, the whole future of the kingdom is darkened by the prospect of an even less sound succession to Henry than was his own to Richard. Hearing of Hotspur's success, Henry is reminded of the sad prospect provided by his son and heir:

> Yea, there thou makest me sad and makest me sin
> In envy that my Lord Northumberland
> Should be the father to so blest a son,
> A son who is the theme of honour's tongue;
> Amongst a grove, the very straightest plant;

Who is sweet Fortune's minion and her pride:
Whilst I, by looking on the praise of him,
See riot and dishonour stain the brow
Of my young Harry. O that it could be proved
That some night-tripping fairy had exchanged
In cradle-clothes our children where they lay, . . .

(I.i.78–88)

The failure in Henry's handling of purely personal relationships is reflected in this impolitic speech, and his later coarse reproaches to his son illustrate the harsh terms that he imposes on those closest to him. It appears that he continues, as king, to force into opposition against him those very qualities of youthful spontaneity that were originally Richard's. Neither Hotspur nor Hal is able to live on friendly terms with him.

As the play develops, Shakespeare demonstrates how the dislocations engendered by Richard's indifference to matters of mere policy have developed and multiplied as the result of Henry's example, so that English society is becoming increasingly disorganized by greed from top to bottom. Not only do the Percys rebel; even the humble carriers on their way to London receive poor service in inns where the very staff themselves arrange plans for highway robbery of the guests. There was nothing visibly unnatural or monstrous about the kingdom of Richard II, but under Henry the evil genius of the new England crystallizes in a Shakespearean figure as characteristic of the times as Richard III had been of the Wars of the Roses: Falstaff.

Falstaff has all the charm and facility of Richard III at his best, coupled with all those faults to which immaturity is prone. His plausibility and greed epitomize the surface self-justification and underlying viciousness that are so widely diffused throughout the land, and that particularly characterize the two elder Percys, Northumberland and Worcester, who use Hotspur as ruthlessly for their ends as Falstaff hopes to use Hal. The robbery organized by Gadshill differs only in scale and grotesqueness from that planned by Worcester; and Hal and Hotspur are both betrayed into dangerous courses, whether it be honor or subtler amusement that they seek. Falstaff is clearly intended to reflect the universal loss of proportion, the triumph of appetites over reason; in this aspect, his role is approximately that of the Vice of the morality plays, as Hal grimly asserts when he acts out the part of his father reprimanding him:

> Thou art violently carried away from grace: there is a devil haunts thee in the likeness of an old fat man; a tun of man is thy companion. Why dost thou converse with that trunk of humours, . . . that reverend Vice, that grey Iniquity, that Father Ruffian, that Vanity in years?

> (II.iv.491–4,498–9)

In many ways this play marks a return to the symbolic methods of *Richard III*, after the comparative realism of *Richard II* and of the main characters of *King John* (with the exception of the Bastard). In the earliest of these three plays we encountered two poles: Richard III and Queen Margaret—respectively, the initiator of evil and the prophetess of its doom. In *Henry IV, Part 1* we see a recurrence of this kind of polarity, now based on the axis of honor, with Falstaff representing complete skepticism at one extreme and Hotspur the opposite excess of utter self-surrender to the pursuit of reputation. This opposition is to be intensified in the second part of the play, in which Falstaff is confronted by the Lord Chief Justice; but in both plays the pivot round which these at least partly symbolic figures revolve is not Henry IV, but his son, Prince Hal. It is clear that Shakespeare does not feel Henry IV himself to be the real center of the sequence, which is concerned with the restoration of the Crown to its true dignity by the rule of a monarch worthier of it than Henry IV, and more politically adept than Richard II. There is thus a subtle shift of emphasis from an exposition of the play of political forces in the earlier phases of the tetralogy, toward a study in the later plays of the evolution and discipline by means of which the ideal ruler is perfected. Essentially this remains a political theme, and numerous hints indicate that it is often at odds with simple ethical judgments. The prince's famous soliloquy at the end of Act I, Scene ii, verges on hypocrisy, while it indicates the complex political evolution through which Hal must proceed in order to avoid a decline such as we saw in Richard's reputation:

> . . . when this loose behaviour I throw off
> And pay the debt I never promised,
> By how much better than my word I am,
> By so much shall I falsify men's hopes;
> And like bright metal on a sullen ground,
> My reformation, glittering o'er my fault,
> Shall show more goodly and attract more eyes
> Than that which hath no foil to set it off.
> (I.ii.231–8)

In this Hal shows himself to be his father's son, exclusively concerned with the political repercussions of even his most intimate relationships.

Sometimes, indeed, he sounds rather canting. He has already dexterously shown up Falstaff's affectation of reform by trapping him into an involuntary assent to participation in a proposed robbery. When the same prospect is offered Hal, he repudiates it with an even more solemn tone than Falstaff's mock reform: "Who, I rob? I a thief? not I, by my faith"—only to be as subtly entrapped by Poins' scheme as Falstaff when betrayed by the Prince's play on his reflexes. The fact is that the Prince's reasons for continuing in this random mode of existence are more complex than he chooses to avow even to himself. On the one hand, he is acquiring a knowledge of the ways and attitudes of an important section of the society that he is ultimately to lead: the lower classes. As he himself implies, he is successfully garnering their good will, just as his father had done on his way into exile:

> I am sworn brother to a leash of drawers; and can call
> them all by their christen names, as Tom, Dick, and
> Francis. They take it already upon their salvation, that
> though I be but Prince of Wales, yet I am the King of
> Courtesy; . . . and when I am King of England, I shall
> command all the good lads of Eastcheap.
>
> (II.iv.6–14)

It was the lack of this kind of popular support that had
undermined Richard's authority as a king, even though he
showed some of Hal's spontaneous delight in a merry life.
Henry's admonition to his son: "As thou art to this hour
was Richard then" (III.ii.94), is only a partial truth, intended to provoke Hal into decorum rather than to fore-
tell his doom as Gaunt had foretold Richard's.

Nevertheless, even if Hal never loses sight of political
reality, ethically he cannot command our respect as much
as his conscious posture might suggest. He is like Richard:
on the threshold of maturity, yet scarcely master of all the
forces at play in and around his personality. What he is
doing, and what he thinks he is doing, are not the same
things. He feels, obviously, that he is indulging his high
spirits: "Well then, once in my days I'll be a madcap"—
and not without an eye for political advantage. But in
practice, as Shakespeare is careful to establish, the Prince's
example is in harmony with the universal decay of English
society under Henry. Gadshill takes satisfaction in such
vindication of crime:

> Tut! there are other Trojans that thou dreamest not
> of, the which for sport sake are content to do the pro-
> fession some grace; that would, if matters should be
> looked into, for their own credit sake, make all whole.
> I am joined with no foot land-rakers, no long-staff six-
> penny strikers, . . . but with nobility and tranquillity.
>
> (II.i.76–83)

Hal not only fosters the criminal elements by assenting to
their crimes, he also corrupts the course of justice, as we
see in his lie to protect the drowsy Falstaff from the

sheriff who comes to arrest him after the robbery (II.iv.561). He also unwisely gives Falstaff a significant command in the royal army. It may be argued that none of Hal's failings is deadly—certainly they involve no such massive disruption of social order as the murder of Woodstock or the seizing of the Lancastrian estate, let alone the usurpation of the throne; but we must recognize that Hal's acts do carry moral and political penalties that he is loath to recognize, and which he meets less by adequate self-vindication than by rationalizations.

It is in the context of these specious arguments for youthful lapses that the personal bearing of Falstaff on Hal's career becomes fully intelligible. Falstaff epitomizes all those symptoms of immaturity to which the potentially superior individual is prone in his early phases: "most subject is the fattest soil to weeds" (*2HIV*, IV.iv.54); and he illustrates how monstrous becomes the survival of such blemishes once maturity has been attained. He also illustrates by what feats of ingenuity such indulgences may be rationalized through his "manner of wrenching the true cause the false way" (*2HIV*, II.i.119). The juxtaposition of Falstaff's physical monstrosity and his mental agility thus becomes subtly symbolic of how the abuse of reason (to which Hal is prone in self-justification) is the natural ally of dubious conduct. Falstaff always has an excellent reason for doing the morally less demanding thing. Furthermore, there are illuminating consequences if we see in Falstaff something like the magnetic fascination of those psychological forces that Freudians (rightly or wrongly) associate with what they call the libido—the instinctual drives that comprise the "id" in each personality, and which only the subtlest analysis can transmute from their repression in the subconsious to control by conscious reason.

Hal's pivotal role commands a universal interest in part because it has inherited the schematic function of the figure, such as Everyman, who represents the human will in the morality plays (what the Freudians might equate with the ego: the conscious part of the mind). In such symbolic terms, other parts of the play fall into place. The sustained tension between Hal and his father is in harmony with modern psychoanalytic theory—Hal resists his father's authority in part because he seeks to supplant it by his own. Not only does Hal seek increasingly to replace his father as effective leader in the field of battle, as at the end of the first part of *Henry IV*, but his involuntary and premature assumption of the crown in the second part (IV.v.21ff.) illustrates perfectly the younger generation's will to supplant the older one, as his father grimly recognizes, accepting this inevitable fact with good grace only after admiring the political finesse of Hal's ingenious self-exculpation.

Even more rewarding is the illumination these ideas cast on the character of Hotspur, which often appears to verge on caricature, particularly in his first scene, with its extravagant cult of honor:

> By heaven methinks it were an easy leap,
> To pluck bright honour from the pale-faced moon,
> Or dive into the bottom of the deep
> Where fathom-line could never touch the ground,
> And pluck up drowned honour by the locks;
> So he that doth redeem her thence might wear
> Without corrival all her dignities.
>   (I.iii.201–7)

Such egotistical speeches (which became notorious to theater people of the time, as we can see by the caricature of this one in *The Knight of the Burning Pestle*) serve to establish Hotspur as the other extreme of immaturity from Falstaff. He illustrates that cult of conventional achievement that inevitably makes Hotspur admired by such morally insensitive minds as Bolingbroke's. It is only in terms of Freudian psychology that Hotspur's attributes begin to cohere in a significant pattern that transcends caricature. His dogmatism, his proneness to rage, and his extravagant cult of traditional emblems of success—all

correlate closely with the Freudian concept of the super-
ego: that quintessence of traditional wisdom that Christians
might prefer to call conscience, but whose authoritarian
(even minatory) aspects are best recognized in psychoanalytic terminology. Blake identified the same characteristics in his version of this moralizing psychic entity:
Urizen. Hal clearly has to make his peace as much with
the perilous obligations implicit in the example of Hotspur
as with the seductive temptations proposed by Falstaff.
The career of Hal lies in his perfecting of the capacity to
strike a mature balance between these conflicting entities
—a balance that Richard II may perhaps have ultimately
attained, but too late for his vindication as a king.

This schematic interpretation of the play defines the
level at which the Shakespearean history play in general
took over the morality tradition. However, it remains only
one of several levels of meaning in *Henry IV*, and it
certainly does not display the full range of Shakespeare's
sensitivity. Neither Flagstaff nor Hotspur is adequately
accounted for in these categorical terms: both twist away
from simple formulations, once the moralistic bearing of
their roles has been established. Hotspur in particular
merits subtler and more sympathetic exposition. If the play
approaches tragedy it is in terms of his experience, and
many of his more complex attributes indicate that it is this
kind of temperament rather than Hal's that is to provide
a model for Othello, Lear, and Antony. No sooner has
Hotspur been established as the norm of traditional bellicosity—cherished and feared by authority, or manipulated by intriguers to serve base purposes—than he is
abruptly presented to us in a new light in Act II, Scene
iii, as the only man in the play to sustain an adequate
relationship with a woman.

The magnificent panegyric Kate speaks over her dead
husband near the start of the second part of *Henry IV* is
one of the most moving moments in that play. The Lancastrian kings never did succeed in calling forth quite that
intensity; in fact, they have very little to do with women,

except perhaps as antagonists. The bluff Hotspur commands his wife's devotion not because of some perverse feminine love of opposition, but rather because, below the level of calculated goals, Hotspur does have reserves of poetry, wisdom, humor, and tenderness that may be too easily overlooked in a schematic analysis of the play as a whole, but are unmistakable in Act II, Scene iii. To his worried wife, distressed by his departure, he there finally extends a considerate reassurance; that offsets his earlier teasing of her:

> . . . hark you, Kate:
> Whither I go, thither shall you go too;
> Today will I set forth, tomorrow you.
> Will this content you, Kate?
> (II.iii.117–20)

It is not by accident that Shakespeare heightens these lines by drawing directly on the famous Biblical passage in which Ruth protests her deep love for Naomi (Ruth, I.16). Here, the words sound like a renewal of the couple's marriage vows.

It is in the first scene of the third act, however, that Hotspur's full complexity appears. There he runs through the whole spectrum of behavior from irascible unpredictability to witty discrimination. He appears at first in a fit of absent-mindedness, having apparently mislaid the papers necessary for the discussion. Thereafter he launches into a quarrel with the Celtic genius Glendower, which is as funny as it is impolitic. Hotspur affects a bluff, Anglo-Saxon contempt for Welsh whimsy and magic, and this confrontation leads to what is perhaps the wittiest single observation in the play. Glendower passionately asserts his power by way of the climactic illustration that he "can call spirits from the vasty deep." To which Hotspur sarcastically replies:

> Why so can I, or so can any man;
> But will they come when you do call for them?
> (III.i.54–5)

The acuteness of mind shown here contrasts with Hotspur's political insensitivity, which is as marked as Richard II's. His maltreatment of Glendower is a plausible explanation for the latter's ultimate failure to arrive at the field of battle at the moment of crisis (the Welsh armies had also abandoned Richard to his fate). Yet, at the same time that he is irritating Glendower, it becomes clear that Hotspur has reserves of incisive judgment and magnetic power that are denied to most of his allies. His brisk (and unresented) ridicule of his wife's affectation of gentility (III.i.230ff.) reflects a solidity of mutual awareness that contrasts memorably with the appalling failure of communication between Mortimer and his Welsh wife, who have to depend on a translator for all their conversation (III.i.192ff.).

Shakespeare makes Hotspur the most gifted person vocally in the whole play: he has a greater range than even Falstaff, since he deploys the resources of the whole rhetorical gamut, from satirical wit to serious political declamation and heroic "braves." We cannot but observe how carefully Shakespeare constructs the character out of conflicting traits, all united by a stroke of paradox. Hotspur suffers from a speech defect, as his wife recalls:

> And speaking thick, which nature made his blemish,
> Became the accents of the valiant;
> For those that could speak low and tardily
> Would turn their own perfection to abuse,
> To seem like him:
> (*2HIV*, II.iii.24–8)

He himself is convinced of his own verbal inadequacy, speaking of himself as one that has "not well the gift of tongue" (V.ii.78). And in his quarrel with Glendower he denounces literary skills:

> I had rather be a kitten and cry mew
> Than one of these same metre ballad-mongers;
> I had rather hear a brazen canstick turn'd,
> Or a dry wheel grate on the axle-tree;

And that would set my teeth nothing on edge,
Nothing so much as mincing poetry:
'Tis like the forced gait of a shuffling nag.
                    (III.i.129–35)

In spite of this, there can be no doubt that Hotspur is the
most skillful rhetorician in the play, almost as alert to
nuances of tone as Falstaff himself. Two of Hotspur's
speeches are among the most eloquent Shakespeare wrote:
the account of the battlefield with the intruding figure of
the court fop (I.iii.29ff.), and the summary of the king's
equivocal career (IV.iii.52ff.). Again and again, Hotspur's
ear recaptures at such moments the nuances of some
speaker's intonation, be it the mincing accents of the fop,
the oily professions of Bolingbroke, or his own wife's too
calculated good manners. Shakespeare has clearly perceived
that such perfection of ear is often the result of compensation: Hotspur's verbal sensitivity and rhetorical command
are, like Sir Winston Churchill's, the products of an awareness that was provoked by a speech defect.

It is already apparent that Hotspur's character is a
complex construct, but it still remains to be recognized
that even his initial role, as a headstrong devotee of the
archaic chivalric code of the Middle Ages, is not crudely
sustained. It is true that before the battle he shows a
tendency to rush into an attack on the king—but for once
he is justified: the steady accumulation of the king's resources argues for a quick assault before they rest and re-
group, as the experienced Douglas agrees. There is an unmistakably suicidal undertone as Hotspur's despair grows:

Doomsday is near; die all, die merrily.
                    (IV.i.134)

But unexpectedly, Hotspur suddenly shows why he is a
good general, even if a bad politician: on the field of
battle, at the moment of crisis, instead of concluding his
dissection of the king's career with a blunt challenge to
battle, he agrees with the king's agent, Blunt, that they
should negotiate. Although he is finally tricked into battle

by his dishonest negotiators, this moment of poised moderation almost at the moment of impact gives to Hotspur an element of unexpected discretion that is perhaps the surest reflection of Shakespeare's genius as a creator of original and complex characters. The characterization of Hotspur ultimately eludes any elementary judgments.

The same complicated response is invited by Falstaff, who even more decisively breaks through the simple convention of the Vice of the morality. If he reflects all the threats that are offered to effective adult behavior by elementary appetites, in this very range of attributes he is closer to the basic rhythm of ordinary life than either the too calculating king or the too volatile Hotspur. In rejecting him, Hal will risk cutting himself off from those human drives that reason aims not to destroy, but to order. In the pre-enactment of Hal's encounter with his father, Falstaff's defense of his own character has a certain authority:

> If sack and sugar be a fault, God help the wicked! if to be old and merry be a sin, then many an old host that I know is damned: if to be fat be to be hated, then Pharaoh's lean kine are to be loved. No, my good lord; banish Peto, banish Bardolph, banish Poins: but for sweet Jack Falstaff, kind Jack Falstaff, true Jack Falstaff, valiant Jack Falstaff, and therefore more valiant, being as he is old Jack Falstaff, banish not him thy Harry's company, banish not him thy Harry's company: banish plump Jack, and banish all the world.
>
> (II.iv.516–27)

The prince's harsh reply "I do, I will" may reflect both the expedient course and the high moralistic line, but it fails to do justice to the complexity of Falstaff's nature and conduct. In the second part of *Henry IV*, by contrast, Falstaff, instead of being narrowly categorized himself, shows that he has mastered the emotional limitations of the Lancastrians, including those of Hal. After the treacherous handling of the rebellion by Hal's brother, Prince

John of Lancaster, Falstaff muses on the family traits that they share:

> Good faith, this same young sober-blooded boy doth not love me; nor a man cannot make him laugh; but that's no marvel, he drinks no wine. . . . Hereof comes it that Prince Henry is valiant; for the cold blood he did naturally inherit of his father, he hath, like lean, sterile and bare land, manured, husbanded and tilled with excellent endeavour of drinking good and good store of sherris, that he is become very hot and valiant.
>
> (*2HIV*, IV.iii.93-6,127-32)

John has no sense of the world and the values that are reflected in Falstaff, while Hal, even if he strenuously repudiates such patterns in the end, still has the virtue of having experienced a broader range of relationships, having also in consequence the capacity to judge others, and himself, more accurately. As Milton is later to say, in *Areopagitica*: "That virtue therefore which is but a youngling in the contemplation of evil, and knows not the utmost that vice promises to her followers, and rejects it, is but a blank virtue, not pure."

Falstaff displays all the resources with which Shakespeare invests his most dangerous characters: verbal skill, wit and humor, a clear sense of his own nature and limitations, and a devastating ability to exploit those of other characters. In fact, it could be argued that Falstaff's power to fascinate is directly related to the fullness of his self-knowledge, which permits him a ready flow of affectations, inoffensive to others because they relate only to himself. This egotism might even seem to be complacent, if the attitudes he affects were not such grotesquely inappropriate ones that they are obviously calculated to defeat belief and provide seductive entertainment. Often (as in his prompt guying of the account of the robbery, as soon as he guesses the identity of the "two rogues in buckram suits"), he invites disbelief in order that he can display the suppleness of an awareness that is in striking contrast to his ungainly body. It is through this extraordinary capacity to "know what he is, and be what he is" (*All's Well*, IV.i.48), without hypocrisy, that Falstaff transcends his formal role. Compared with most of those around him (Hotspur, most conspicuously), Falstaff is one major step nearer Christian salvation in that he recognizes his own defects, even if he uses this knowledge chiefly as a source for wittily ironic pretensions to excellence. It is striking how steady a pressure for self-awareness Falstaff exerts on the Prince, as we see most significantly in the rehearsal of the confrontation between Hal and his father. What Falstaff fosters in such scenes is an awareness of the private self's capacity for good or evil. His own moral failings are mostly on the plane of private morality rather than on that of public or political action, in whose operations he plays little direct part.

Of the two poles of moral attitude displayed by Falstaff and Hotspur, Falstaff's is by far the less disastrous, and even gains vindication from the play's action. Falstaff's policy of fighting no "longer than he sees reason" (I.ii.206) comes nearer to the play's norm of behavior than does Hotspur's daring. Hotspur has no reserves to fall back on, once his main line of policy proves inadequate, while Falstaff's secondary lines of defense are endless. This greater psychological resilience on the part of Falstaff finds physical vindication in the final battle scenes, where Falstaff symbolically triumphs over the dead Hotspur, by not only "miraculously" rising from the dead, but even claiming Hotspur's military renown for his own. Indeed, the question of Falstaff's valor cannot properly be debated within this context, for the play unequivocally repudiates Hotspur's view of bravery and leadership, while it validates something very like Falstaff's in the most practical ways. Whatever one may think of Falstaff's tattered regiment of outcasts, it does actually reach the field of battle on time, in this respect clearly surpassing the levies (however well-equipped) of Glendower and Mortimer, who in this crucial matter prove to be inferior officers to Falstaff.

It is in the juxtaposition with Douglas, however, that Falstaff's code finds its fullest vindication. Douglas' military prowess is firmly recognized by both sides as being of the highest order. Hal orders his release without ransom after he has been captured, because:

> His valour shown upon our crests to-day
> Hath taught us how to cherish such high deeds
> Even in the bosom of our adversaries.
> (V.v.29–31)

One notes how dexterously Hal recapitulates his father's calculated generosity to some foes, but the politic praise here merely corroborates Hotspur's earlier testimony (IV.i.1ff.). Yet how does Douglas, this paragon of military virtue, actually behave? He shows none of Hotspur's death-courting ambition:

> Talk not of dying: I am out of fear
> Of death or death's hand for this one-half year.
> (IV.i.135–6)

He feels not unlike Falstaff who, on seeing the dead Sir Walter Blunt, exclaims "I like not such grinning honour as Sir Walter hath." Douglas indeed had earlier insulted his misidentified victim in even harsher terms:

> "A fool" go with thy soul, whither it goes!
> A borrow'd title hast thou bought too dear:
> Why didst thou tell me that thou wert a king?
> (V.iii.22–4)

The mention of this fatal disguise, which has helped to protect the real King Henry, reminds us that others besides Falstaff, and of far nobler position, have also resorted to "counterfeits" in order to preserve their lives. The most striking analogy to Falstaff's code is to be found, however, in Hal's account of the capture of Douglas:

> The noble Scot, Lord Douglas, when he saw
> The fortune of the day quite turn'd from him,
> The noble Percy slain, and all his men

Upon the foot of fear, fled with the rest;
And falling from a hill, he was so bruised
That the pursuers took him.
                    (V.v.17–22)

There is little here that can be distinguished from Falstaff's
physical clumsiness and his policy of fighting no longer
"than he sees reason," yet Hal still goes on to praise
Douglas for "valour." Falstaff's "cowardice" thus comes
nearer to the broadly accepted norms of conduct in the
play than the bravery of Hotspur or Blunt, which has
something suicidal about it. It is interesting to note that
Hal's one gesture in this direction, the challenge of Hotspur to single combat, is flatly turned down by the king,
as might be expected. Hal can afford the gesture, since he
must know that the life of the heir–apparent could
scarcely be risked so lightly, for "considerations infinite /
Do make against it" (V.i.102–3).

In these last scenes, Hal moves efficiently through the
various phases of the battle, illustrating his new mastery of
resources displayed by other characters earlier in the play.
He manages not only to fight better than Hotspur, but to
maneuver as cunningly as the king and Worcester. His
gesture of sacrificing to Falstaff the honor of killing
Hotspur is perhaps his subtlest stroke of self-discipline.
He thereby defeats the temptations offered both by Falstaff's opportunism and Hotspur's cult of glory—distract-
ing the former's attention with the idea of his apparent
humiliating triumph over the latter. No doubt such patterns
could be allegorized moralistically, but even though the
play is primarily concerned with the development of a
truly kingly personality, the central issues remain political,
rather than ethical. The victory of the king, however
precariously dependent it may be on such figures as
Falstaff, must be measured against the principle of Richard
III: that the Crown cannot effectively be challenged so
long as it is effectively possessed.

It is certain that both King John and King Henry IV
survive the attacks on their authority in part because they

effectively sustain the role of the national government when it is beset by foreign powers (be they French, Welsh, or Scots) that are allied with traitors. However unworthy the wearer of the crown (and the King makes no effort to answer the Percys' charges), he has at least an administrative advantage, and probably a psychological one too, if he makes any serious effort to exert it. Worcester recognizes this:

> For well you know we of the offering side
> Must keep aloof from strict arbitrement,
> And stop all right-holes, every loop from whence
> The eye of reason may pry in upon us.
> (IV.i.69–72)

Later the Archbishop of York recognizes the natural momentum of central authority, which the king exploits as he gathers "The special head of all the land together" (IV.iv.27).

When we consider the dubious moral character of the forces on both sides, their unpredictability, and their low morale (implicit in the unwillingness of either side to begin the battle), it must be apparent that it is above all the titular authority of Henry as king that gives him the advantage over Worcester. The very appearance of legality lends the stability of inertia to the state that the Percys seek to overthrow. Without any significant advantage, such as the absence of the monarch—as in the case of Richard II—rebellion has, in Shakespeare's mind, little hope of success. If the throne is empty, or "the sword unsway'd," then alone can rebellion hope to detach the loyalty of the populace from the established government. Not only will Falstaff, for all his amorality, submit to titular authority even while seeking to exploit it for his own advantage, but the headstrong Hotspur will negotiate with it, at the very moment of the battle that he has himself desired. The reign of Henry IV thus vindicates the status of the Crown, which his own accession had seemed to invalidate.

3

Henry IV
Part Two

THE DIFFICULTIES involved in dislodging even a mediocre (but established) government are also brought out in the second part of *Henry IV*, which dispenses with almost all the physical elements of rebellion and instead investigates its purely psychological aspects. This emphasis appears from the start, in the figure of the Prologue, "Rumour, painted full of tongues":

> . . . who but Rumour, who but only I,
> Make fearful musters and prepared defence,
> Whiles the big year, swoln with some other grief,
> Is thought with child by the stern tyrant war,
> And no such matter?

(Induction, 11-15)

However, the first effects of false military intelligence on the vacillating Northumberland are less significant than the counterpoint that develops later between the views of the representatives of the central government and the specious arguments by which the Archbishop of York (like Pandulph in *King John*) seeks to justify rebellion against the Crown. The very arguments with which the Bishop of Carlisle had seriously discountenanced Bolingbroke before his assumption of the crown in *Richard II* (IV.i.114ff.) no longer seem to carry the same conviction, now that Bolingbroke appears effectively to possess it.

The rebels in *2 Henry IV*, fail to recognize this reversal, and are firmly convinced, like the nobles who helped the French against King John, that moral sanctions easily override political pressures. Mowbray observes to Northumberland that Hotspur's defeat reflected the chilling overtones of the word "rebellion":

> But now the bishop
> Turns insurrection to religion: . . .
> Derives from heaven his quarrel and his cause;
> Tells them he doth bestride a bleeding land,
> Gasping for life under great Bolingbroke.
> (I.i.200–1,206–8)

It is no accident that this political exploitation of religious motivations should coincide with observations made by Machiavelli. Even though *The Prince* had not been printed in English, and the theater was familiar with its author's political philosophy only in such fantastic illustrations of it as Richard III, there is no doubt that the original text was known to many politicians who served the later Tudors. The usurpation of the titular headship of the Anglican church by the sovereign, which Henry VIII promulgated, was entirely in harmony with Machiavelli's reflections on the maintenance, by theological pressures, of the temporal authority of Moses and the Papacy.

However, Mowbray's recognition of the Archbishop's role as the vindicator of the morality of rebellion is carefully counterweighted by the nihilistic statement of Northumberland that precedes Mowbray's speech by only a few lines. In a crisis of despair, Northumberland has invoked the destruction of the world in terms as appalling as any that Lear or Macbeth will use in their blackest moments:

> Let heaven kiss earth! now let not Nature's hand
> Keep the wild flood confined! let order die!
> And let this world no longer be a stage
> To feed contention in a lingering act;
> But let one spirit of the first-born Cain
> Reign in all bosoms, that, each heart being set

On bloody courses, the rude scene may end,
And darkness be the burier of the dead!
                    (I.i.153–60)

It is with such diabolical nihilism that Shakespeare subtly
associates the Archbishop's specious moralizing in the second part of *Henry IV*.

Even these pious reflections themselves have a curiously
self-incriminating quality:

> . . . we are all diseased,
> And with the surfeiting and wanton hours
> Have brought ourselves into a burning fever,
> And we must bleed for it; of which disease
> Our late king, Richard, being infected, died.
> But, my most noble Lord of Westmoreland,
> I take not on me here as a physician,
> Nor do I as an enemy to peace
> Troop in the throngs of military men;
> But rather show awhile like fearful war,
> To diet rank minds sick of happiness
> And purge the obstructions which begin to stop
> Our very veins of life.
>   (IV.i.54–66)

This tendency to see the state as an organism (an image
that Hobbes is to develop in *Leviathan*, as its very name
suggests), is quite characteristic of the later Shakespearean
history plays. The complex but coherent interplay of
moral issues, and the almost legalistic correspondence of
actions and penalties that in the earlier plays had reflected
the precepts, if not the direct interventions of Providence,
now derive their logic from the temporal vicissitudes of
the body politic.

An infection affects all parts of a body to some degree,
whatever its more local origin. And like the macrocosm
of the body politic, Henry himself is also afflicted throughout the play with a chronic illness that colors his speeches,
so that they also invite association with the Archbishop's
political diagnosis. After describing his sleepless nights,
the King discusses the bad news with his followers:

Then you perceive the body of our kingdom
How foul it is; what rank diseases grow,
And with what danger near the heart of it.
(III.i.38–40)

The pattern of allusion also extends even to that symbol of the kingdom's anarchy, Falstaff himself. In *Part 1*, Falstaff was physically gross, but he preserved an unquestioned vitality. In the sequel, he appears from the start on the verge of that final collapse whose description by Hostess is to form one of the most poignant scenes in *Henry V* (II.iii).

Falstaff enters (I.ii.1ff.) discussing a doctor's diagnosis of a urine sample he had sent him. Immediately afterwards, he is confronted by the ruthless exposition of his physical senility by the Lord Chief Justice (I.ii.200ff.), later corroborated by Falstaff's resentment of Hal's jests on this account (II.iv.4ff.). Even the sentimental exchanges with Doll Tearsheet are darkly colored by forebodings: "Peace, good Doll! do not speak like a death's-head; do not bid me remember mine end" (II.iv.254–5). It is significant that Falstaff's exploits in the earlier play implied more than a little physical agility, both in the robbery and on the battlefield. Now, by contrast, his travels in Gloucestershire display only administrative abuses of military propriety: the misuse of the king's commission to impress soldiers, which leads to the abuse of Shallow's hospitality by confidence tricks, put over under the color of Falstaff's expectations in the new reign. Falstaff cannot be expected to recognize that, as the symbol for the abuses of the state under Henry IV, he can hardly count on surviving in an era that cancels all the warrants of the older generation but those whose characteristics anticipated the new, such as the fierce integrity of the Lord Chief Justice who threw the Prince into jail for contempt of court.

However, it is the political aspects of the play's plot that provide the most shocking illustration of the disintegration of healthy standards of conduct. It is obvious that even on the local level justice has decayed under the loose administration of magistrates such as Shallow, who have become mere tools of clever underlings. Davy, for example, does not scruple to manipulate his master shamelessly: "If I cannot once or twice in a quarter bear out a knave against an honest man, I have but a very little credit with your worship" (V.i.53-5). This kind of abuse of office is only one symptom among many. Not only does Falstaff hope to achieve Davy's role on a national scale through his influence with Hal; even the titular leaders of society do not hesitate to sacrifice their integrity to expediency—all the while professing a virtue to which they have little claim.

The play's central historical episode is the disintegration of the rebellion led by the Archbishop of York. Here the shadowiness of the society now presented to us appears in the feeble contrasts that it makes with even the anarchistic vitality and charm of the preceding play. There is not a single courageous blow struck in the whole later encounter; one leader of the rebellion, Coleville, surrenders (IV.iii) to the mere shadow that is Falstaff's reputation (based, as we know, on the misreport of his victory over Hotspur). The specious arguments of the archbishop are met by the acceptance of the king's representative, John of Lancaster, Hal's younger brother. The kingdom has sunk into such moral apathy that any means to secure peace now appears to be justified (much as Hobbes was later to feel). Prince John meets the Archbishop's inevitable reproaches for treachery with frigid sophistries, clearly backed by his inflexible will to preserve the vestiges of effective government at any political price:

> I promised you redress of these same grievances
> Whereof you did complain; which, by mine honour,
> I will perform with a most Christian care.
> But for you, rebels, look to taste the due
> Meet for rebellion and such acts as yours.
> Most shallowly did you these arms commence,
> Fondly brought here and foolishly sent hence.
> Strike up our drums, pursue the scatter'd fray:

God, and not we, hath safely fought today.
Some guard these traitors to the block of death,
Treason's true bed and yielder up of breath.
(IV.ii.113–23)

Prince John shows no awareness of the fact that just such
a fate had been merited by his father's own rebellion. The
possession of this awareness may perhaps explain the unexpected moderation of his father to such earlier rebels as
Aumerle, the Bishop of Carlisle, and the Percys. But John
has no trace of that gallantry that was characteristic of
Richard II at his best, and which Hal so deftly borrows
(while enhancing it) from Hotspur.

John's cutting political judgment belongs to the modern
world rather than to that half mythical medieval world
to which Hotspur's chivalry regresses. It is significant that
Hal's judgment increasingly tends toward John's pattern
as the play evolves. Late in the play Falstaff is still praising
Hal for his "excellent endeavour of drinking," which has
offset this frigid disposition so apparent in John, and made
him "very hot and valiant" (IV.iii.132). But the fact is
that Falstaff's judgment is progressively falsified from Hal's
first appearance in the play (II.ii.1ff.). This is marked by
a sustained bitterness against his fellow roisterers, such as
had only intermittently appeared in the first part of *Henry
IV*. Toping increasingly disgusts him: he asks Poins, "Doth
it not show vilely in me to desire small beer?" (II.ii.6).
Only a few lines later the revulsion extends to Poins himself: "What a disgrace is it to me to remember thy name!
or to know thy face tomorrow!" He is the more dissatis-
fied in that his behavior has denied him the opportunity
for public expression of his own better instincts: "I tell
thee my heart bleeds inwardly that my father is so sick:
and keeping such vile company as thou art hath in reason
taken from me all ostentation of sorrow" (II.i.51–4). The
tone is ungracious, and in the wish for the "ostentation of
sorrow" we see that he is, after all, his father's son, longing
to strike the public attitude. The fact remains that he has
been trapped in the role of the inverted hypocrite: one

who seeks to appear worse than he is. This repression of traditional feelings has built up in him an accumulation of moral energy that is triggered by the first opportunity to hurry himself away from his half-hearted teasing of Falstaff:

> By heaven, Poins, I feel me much to blame,
> So idly to profane the precious time,
> When tempest of commotion, like the south
> Borne with black vapour, doth begin to melt
> And drop upon our bare unarmed heads.
> Give me my sword and cloak. Falstaff, good night.
>
> (II.iv.390–5)

It is true that in the previous play Hal had already taken the initiative from his father on the field of battle. The field command is now delegated to the younger brother, John. Hal's ambitions, by contrast, are no longer fixed on displays of mere physical prowess, or on military maneuvers, but on securing his effective succession to his father. This is perhaps the climactic theme of the action in this part of the tetralogy: the nature of succession inevitably preoccupies the dying, sleepless Henry IV—in part as a reflection of the king's own guilty conscience:

> Uneasy lies the head that wears the crown.
>
> (III.i.31)

Unlike those of Northumberland, however, his apocalyptic visions are less nihilistic, although scarcely less terrifying:

> O God! that one might read the book of fate,
> And see the revolution of the times
> Make mountains level, and the continent,
> Weary of solid firmness, melt itself
> Into the sea! and, other times, to see
> The beachy girdle of the ocean
> Too wide for Neptune's hips; how chances mock,
> And changes fill the cup of alteration
> With divers liquors! O, if this were seen,
> The happiest youth, viewing his progress through

What perils past, what crosses to ensue,
Would shut the book, and sit him down and die.
(III.i.45-56)

There is no doubt that the dislocations of natural order
that Henry apprehensively visualizes for the future are
projections of those reversals of social order in which he
has played so large a part—albeit, in his view, an unintended one. He asserts that Richard unfairly accused him
of seeking the throne, even as late as the time of the deposed king's attack on Northumberland, when the latter
carried Richard off from his queen (V.i.55):

Though then, God knows, I had no such intent,
But that necessity so bow'd the state
That I and greatness were compell'd to kiss.
(III.i.72-4)

Examination of the earlier play readily shows the falseness
of this assertion—a falseness that Shakespeare clearly intended this passage to make explicit, perhaps less as a
symptom of the king's declining mind, than of his almost
automatic concern for appearances. While Henry specu-
lates over the lack of foresight he now feels in himself, as
compared with the prophetic power by which the doomed
Richard foretold the kingdom's future miseries, Westmoreland takes a purely naturalistic view of Richard's
visionary insights. He attributes them to a pattern "figuring
the nature of the times deceased," from which "a man may
prophesy" indeed, but only because he happens to make
"a perfect guess" (III.i.8off.). The aura of spiritual authority that invested Gaunt on his deathbed, and lingered
round the declining Richard, now appears to be only the
result of dearly bought experience. Metaphysical sanctions
and prophetic inspiration have alike disappeared from the
secularized world of the Lancastrian kings.

In these more mundane terms, Henry is not without
insight into the character of his successor, although his
guess about his son's career is wide of the mark. He realizes
that Hal is far more extreme and variable in character than

himself, and therefore has greater potentialities for both
good and evil:

> He hath a tear for pity and a hand
> Open as day for melting charity:
> Yet notwithstanding, being incensed, he's flint,
> As humorous as winter and as sudden
> As flaw congealed in the spring of day.
> His temper, therefore, must be well observed.
> (IV.iv.31–6)

There are elements of many kinds of personality here:
Richard's more charming traits mingled with a severity
that Richard rarely displayed. The advice that Hal "be
well observed" stems less from the purposes of flattery
than from the fear of his latent ruthlessness. Hal is more
widely experienced than either his father or his father's
predecessor, but his personality is thereby made even less
accessible to conventional restraints than was that of his
superficially rather conventional father, who apprehensively anticipates the time

> When I am sleeping with my ancestors.
> For when his headstrong riot hath no curb,
> When rage and hot blood are his counsellors,
> When means and lavish manners meet together,
> O with what wings shall his affections fly
> Towards fronting peril and opposed decay!
> (IV.iv.61–6)

The implicit analogy to Richard II is, of course, false. It is
Richard's misfortune to have occupied the throne before
he had come to know the full gamut of experience—both
the good and the bad—as a private person. Thus his inevitable lapses carry major political penalties that Hal's
peccadilloes never invite. Warwick reiterates the educative
value of Hal's experience (IV.iv.67–78), along the lines
of Hal's earliest soliloquy; but useful as these advantages
are, the major consequence of his escapades is that Hal
is already bored by such lesser pleasures before he becomes king, and is excited by the prospect of the satis-

factions of authority in a way that Richard never did have the opportunity to be.

We have already seen Hal's boredom with his old haunts reflected in a malice directed against their habitués. The famous scene in which he anticipates his father's death by prematurely seizing the crown reflects his ambition to meet weightier challenges than those afforded by bouts of wit with Falstaff. In many ways he rightly feels that the crown has proven to be too demanding a burden for his father's personality: Henry IV never has an opportunity to assume the initiative as king, despite his oft-deferred desire to make a crusade. His all too limited spiritual resources are depleted in merely maintaining his authority (IV.iv.117-20), and it is with something like despair that the king recognizes his own increasing incapacity, and the effective supersession of his authority by younger men's successes:

> And wherefore should these good news make me
>   sick? . . .
> I should rejoice now at this happy news;
> And now my sight fails, and my brain is giddy:
> O me! come near me; now I am much ill.
>   (IV.iv.102,109–11)

The prince's action in removing the crown from his father's supposed deathbed appears to be the ultimate challenge, and accounts for the venom of the king's attack on his son:

> Pluck down my officers, break my decrees;
> For now a time is come to mock at form:
> Harry the Fifth is crown'd: up, vanity! . . .
> Now, neighbour confines, purge you of your scum:
> Have you a ruffian that will swear, drink, dance,
> Revel the night, rob, murder, and commit
> The oldest sins the newest kind of ways?
> Be happy he will trouble you no more; . . .
> For the Fifth Harry from curb'd license plucks
> The muzzle of restraint, and the wild dog
> Shall flesh his tooth on every innocent.
>   (IV.v.118–20,124–8,131–3)

This is as virulent as that earlier encounter in which the king accused his son of a willingness to join the rebels against the new monarchy. The previous challenge seems to have been governed, however, by a calculated weighing of the prince's basic integrity, which his father attempts to provoke into heroic virtue.

On this later occasion, the king is less deliberate in his insults, but the effect remains the same. In reply, the prince scarcely answers the charges directly; instead, he displays a rhetorical finesse that strikes a responsive chord in the dying king, to whom it recalls his own devious rise. Thus Henry can now see in his son a political potential even more significant than the martial prowess that Hal had shown against Hotspur—and he hastens to rationalize those pious aspirations of his own to head a crusade in a few last, breathless words of political advice to his successor:

> Yet, though thou stand'st more sure than I could do,
> Thou art not firm enough, since griefs are green;
> And all my friends, which thou must make thy friends,
> Have but their stings and teeth newly ta'en out;
> By whose fell working I was first advanced
> And by whose power I well might lodge a fear
> To be again displaced: which to avoid,
> I cut them off; and had a purpose now,
> To lead out many to the Holy Land,
> Lest rest and lying still might make them look
> Too near unto my state. Therefore, my Harry,
> Be it thy course to busy giddy minds
> With foreign quarrels; that action, hence borne out,
> May waste the memory of the former days.
>   (IV.v.203–16)

Here lies the ultimate revelation of Henry's thoughts: he displays a mind that is sensitive only to political pressures, and is utterly devoid of any of those finer emotions and instincts that unbalance figures like Duke Humphrey, Richard II, and Hotspur. For Henry, the idea of "friends" carries little more than a sense of political association, motivated by as ruthless an egotism as any Hobbes could possibly have conceived. He also admits that his Crusade was designed primarily to distract attention from his own guilt, and advises his son to seek no less seductive distractions for his antagonists during his own reign.

There is a marked contrast between the naked cynicism of this moment in the legitimate transfer of authority from Henry to his son, and the high drama of Henry's own encounter with the abdicating Richard. It was Richard's misfortune never to have seen the divergence between his formal public role and the realities of politics and of individual motivation; it is Henry's misfortune never to have been able to achieve any adequate coordination between his almost invisible private personality and his public *persona*. Henry represents a far more dreary and naturalistic version of that schizophrenia that Shakespeare had heightened to diabolical intensity in the figure of Richard III.

This then is Hal's introduction to the seat of power in the government. It is too disabusing and too absolute in its admonitions for us to expect the characterization of Henry V to be in essence what it seems to be. Hal had long before announced that his relationship with Falstaff was not what it seemed, so that he inherits from his father both an inherent reserve about his more inward motivations, and a code of monarchy that refuses any credit to private instincts. The discrepancy between the Crown and the individual who wears it has been fully mastered by these Lancastrians. The question remains: how far can this disjunction serve the best interests of the state, while not undermining the individual's sense of his own moral responsibility for his actions, as it did in the case of Richard III? This question not only concerns Shakespeare in *Henry V*, but is raised to a higher level of abstraction in one of his sonnets, which seems likely to have been written with just such situations in mind:

They that have power to hurt and will do none,
That do not do the thing they most do show,
Who, moving others, are themselves as stone,

Unmoved, cold and to temptation slow,
They rightly do inherit heaven's graces
And husband nature's riches from expense;
They are the lords and owners of their faces,
Others but stewards of their excellence.
                    (*Sonnet 94*, 1–8)

The latent hypocrisy of the sort of personality that is
sketched in these lines has been a subject for unfavorable
comment; but we must note that the spontaneous charm
and willfulness of a Richard II or a Hotspur lead no less
to disorder and destruction than do far more villainous
motivations, such as those of King John or the Macbeths.
When calculation is utterly divorced from the springs of
humane values as it all too often is in *Henry IV*, then
anarchy must result, just as it perpetually verges on doing
in *King John*, to be averted only by the happy interventions of the Bastard, who restores a truer balance of instinct and calculation to John's administration.

Does Henry V strike a similar balance in his reign? By
the end of *Henry IV*, all we can say is that he shows a
manipulative capacity equal to his father's, and even remi-
niscent of that subtle testing of his victims' personality into
which Richard III had refined the role of the Vice. Henry
V's first significant act is to challenge the discretion of the
Lord Chief Justice who had previously punished him and
censured Falstaff. The challenge implies a hostility that
tempts the Justice to repent publicly for his earlier severity, a temptation that he forthrightly resists, only to learn
thereupon that the king really agrees with his earlier severity, and has feigned indignation only in order to test the
integrity of the man whom he now confirms in his high
office. The episode shows that from the start Henry V is
able to discriminate between what he seems to be doing
(here, reproaching the Justice) and what he is really doing
(vindicating the Justice's integrity). No act of Henry can
be judged at face value after this striking reversal of expectation.

There is a sinister ambiguity in the apparently gracious

conclusion to his otherwise merciless public repudiation of Falstaff in the last scene of the play:

> For competence of life I will allow you,
> That lack of means enforce you not to evil:
> And as we hear you do reform yourselves,
> We will, according to your strengths and qualities,
> Give you advancement. Be it your charge, my lord,
> To see perform'd the tenour of our word.
>
> (V.v.70–5)

It is with something like shock that we shortly thereafter hear the order of the Lord Chief Justice, to whom the king has entrusted the discharge of his judgment: Falstaff and his followers are to be jailed in the Fleet Prison. It may be accidental that the king's word, "tenour," is ambiguous; certainly it would appear that it is only by exploiting the word's less well-known legal sense of "a literal transcription" (as opposed to "the general meaning") that the Justice could manage to twist the king's apparent graciousness into so grim, yet nominally precise, an interpretation. For imprisonment would be one way of providing "competence of life," and "reform" does suggest discipline. However, we have some evidence that what is involved is not simply the perverse legalism of a judge, but the predictable realization of the king's harsh intentions, according to the Lancastrian dispensation. Prince John gives us the grounds for believing this, in voicing to the Lord Chief Justice his sardonic approval of the judge's severe interpretation of the king's words:

> I like this fair proceeding of the king's:
> He hath intent his wonted followers
> Shall all be very well provided for.
>
> (V.v.103–5)

One might still be inclined to consider that even this comment implied a happier outcome for Falstaff and his friends, until we recall John's dislike of Falstaff (IV.iii.90ff.), and how ruthlessly legalistic John has already proven himself to be in his policy of observing no more than the letter of the truce he has made with the naive rebels. For none of the Lancastrians can be trusted as men: what Hotspur had bitterly observed of the previous monarch is no less true of Henry V:

> The king is kind; and well we know the king
> Knows at what time to promise, when to pay.
> (*1HIV*, IV.iii.52–3)

As Prince of Wales, Henry V had long ago privately promised himself a drastic break with Falstaff, and had also made other promises, which Falstaff had even then misunderstood (*1HIV*, I.ii.74,218). The rough justice meted out to his erstwhile companion thus follows the prince's original intention of brusquely breaking the pattern of his life. It also matches the coarse discipline exacted by the precarious authority of his father in England when he executed Bushy and Green on specious charges and without strict title (*RII*, III.i). The Lancastrians cannot afford that luxury of reasoning with dangerous elements in their state that Richard II had once enjoyed. The new king has indeed undergone a more worthy succession than his father, but his ultimate title is still as doubtful as his father's. The Wars of the Roses are to make this disastrously clear throughout his own son's long and tragic reign as Henry VI, a reign that Shakespeare so fully explored in his first tetralogy.

The misfortune that a minor was elevated to the throne thus marks the start of the disintegration of medieval England under Richard II, a process that the last of the Lancastrians, Henry VI, consummates for the same reasons: he is a youthful and inexperienced monarch succeeding prematurely to an illustrious father. The prime political theme that remains to be explored in *Henry V* is whether such a curse as Richard brought on England can ever be offset by a later, more mature ruler, and how far the attributes of such a hero's reign can constitute an ideal performance, rather than merely reflecting the bellicosity that is usually resorted to by any insecure state. In the light of its Shakespearean context—looking to *Henry VI*, as well as to *Richard II*—*Henry V* may well prove to be a more complex play than is ordinarily recognized. Its simple epic line masks a skillful policy devised by a subtle ruler with an elusive personality. Henry V is indeed Shakespeare's "ideal king," but the term proves to be less positive than one might expect.

4

Henry V

"No, MY GOOD LORD; banish Peto, banish Bardolph, banish Poins: but for sweet Jack Falstaff, kind Jack Falstaff, true Jack Falstaff, valiant Jack Falstaff, and therefore more valiant, being, as he is, old Jack Falstaff, banish not him thy Harry's company, banish not him thy Harry's company: banish plump Jack, and banish all the world." To this impassioned speech of Falstaff's in the first part of *Henry IV* (II.iv.520–7), Hal had replied less than playfully: "I do, I will"—prefiguring the ultimate repudiation of his fat friend and all that he stands for, both good and bad. It has not been adequately recognized that Falstaff's absence from *Henry V* makes as distinctive a contribution to its atmosphere as did his presence to *Henry IV*. This is not to say that the later play is thinner than its predecessors by the lack of his comic figure, but rather the reverse: the eclipse of many humane elements in the new king's personality is stressed by the way in which Falstaff's spirit haunts the play's dark texture, providing a necessary norm of reference in our response to Henry's "new" personality.

Henry's resolute harshness is evidenced by new black threads in the weave of the play, alongside the high colors of a few of the figures in its foreground. In view of this *chiaroscuro*, the play proves to be less simply epic than has usually been assumed, and to have somewhat more in common with the anti-epic overtones of *Troilus and Cressida*. In the first part of *Henry IV*, there had been relatively few sinister effects, apart from Worcester's treachery to Hotspur. In the second part, we have a far more overtly diseased society, with the addition of the prostitute Doll Tearsheet to replace the attractive Lady Percy. In *Henry V*, this pattern of development reaches that harsh extreme that is to give its coloration, intermittently at least, to such plays as *Measure for Measure*, *King Lear*, and *Timon of Athens*, in which the images of venereal disease continually recur, along lines first crudely sketched by Pistol's acid advice to Nym, his rival for the hand of the Hostess:

> . . . to the spital go,
> And from the powdering-tub of infamy
> Fetch forth the lazar kite of Cressid's kind,
> Doll Tearsheet she by name, and her espouse:
> I have, and I will hold, the quondam Quickly.
>   (II.i.78–82)

Later, Pistol also announces:

> News have I, that my Nell is dead i' the spital
> Of malady of France;
> And there my rendezvous is quite cut off.
>   V.i.86–8)

Not only is such English femininity as appears in the play thus shown to be fatally debauched, but the French-women of the highest rank are shown to conceal a treasonous lust for English virility beneath their affectation of prudery. We may feel that there is simply chivalric exaggeration in the Dauphin's account of the plight of the French nobility, who have been accepting the English invasion passively. He claims:

> By faith and honour,
> Our madams mock at us, and plainly say
> Our mettle is bred out and they will give
> Their bodies to the lust of English youth
> To new-store France with bastard warriors.
>   (III.v.27–31)

However, it is not by accident that only a few lines earlier, the French princess, Katherine, has herself been assiduously learning English; and while she pretends disgust at the sexual associations of some of the English words (III.iii.54-8), this physiological awareness itself unmistakably indicates that she rightly expects, one way or another, to be exposed to the embraces of the English. The later scene of her surrender to Henry's courtship curiously echoes that of the seduction of Lady Anne by Richard III, for the French princess manages to overcome an analogous barrier of loyalty ("Is it possible dat I sould love de enemy of France?" [V.ii.178]) by accepting a specious logic, which Henry shares with Richard:

No; it is not possible you should love the enemy of France, Kate: but in loving me, you should love the friend of France; for I love France so well that I will not part with a village of it; I will have it all mine; and, Kate, when France is mine and I am yours, then yours is France and you are mine.

(V.ii.180-5)

This reveals the virtuosity of argument that Hal had learned from Falstaff, in such exchanges as the one in which Falstaff was challenged as to whether the prince owed him a thousand pounds as he had claimed, and replied: "A thousand pound, Hal! a million: thy love is worth a million: thou owest me thy love" (1HIV, III.iii.154-5). An even more authentic echo of Falstaff occurs when the Boy exclaims at the battle of Harfleur: "Would I were in an alehouse in London! I would give all my fame for a pot of ale and safety" (III.ii.12-3). It is typical of the sinister tone of Henry V that the Boy and all his youthful fellows are slain by the "chivalric" French in revenge for their defeat at Agincourt by Henry V, "wherefore the king most worthily, hath caused every soldier to cut his prisoner's throat. O, 'tis a gallant king!" (IV.vii.9-11) After such an episode one may begin to sympathize with Fluellen's dry scholarly analogies be-

tween Henry and the ancient hero whom he clumsily calls
"Alexander the Pig" (IV.vii.14).

To Gower's inevitable correction "Alexander the
Great," he sharply replies:

> Why, I pray you, is not pig great? the pig, or the
> great, or the mighty, or the huge, or the magnanimous,
> are all one reckonings, save the phrase is a little varia-
> tions.
>
> (IV.vii.16–19)

Nevertheless, although by now we understand that "pig"
is a Welsh mispronunciation of "big," the passage has
somewhat thrown out of balance our response to reputation; that this is intended appears in Fluellen's account of
Alexander, which fully justifies the "accidental" bestial
association:

> If you mark Alexander's life well, Harry of Mon-
> mouth's is come after it indifferent well: for there are
> figures in all things. Alexander, God knows, and you
> know, in his rages and his furies, and his wraths, and
> his cholers, and his moods, and his displeasures, and his
> indignations, and also being a little intoxicates in his
> prains, did, in his ales and his angers, look you, kill his
> best friend, Cleitus.
>
> (IV.vii.32–41)

To Gower's prim rejoinder: "Our king is not like him in
that: he never killed any of his friends," the pedantical
Fluellen (perhaps drawn after Shakespeare's Welsh school-
master) replies indignantly that he is being unfairly interrupted, and explains:

> I speak but in the figures and comparisons of it: Alex-
> ander killed his friend Cleitus, being in his ales and his
> cups; so also Harry Monmouth, being in his right wits
> and good judgments, turned away the fat knight with
> the great-belly doublet: he was full of jests, and gipes,
> and knaveries, and mocks; I have forgot his name.
>
> (IV.vii.45–53)

This permits Gower to stress Falstaff's name in reply, and the king's immediate entrance vindicates Fluellen's comparison to Alexander by Henry's first lines:

I was not angry since I came to France
Until this instant.
  (IV.vii.58–9)

The anger, of course, rises from the killing of the English boys, but it has resulted in the murder of all the French prisoners. Nor can we cherish the suggestion that Henry did in cold blood to Falstaff what Alexander, intoxicated, had done to Cleitus.

There is at least one other significant scene that reinforces Falstaff's changed role in *Henry V*, a scene in which he appears to illustrate many of the more intimate and less political values that Henry's public role requires him to sacrifice. Even before Falstaff's death, the Hostess has poignantly observed: "The king has killed his heart" (II.i.92). And in the moving account of his death, we must note that, through her garbled version of his last words, there appear clear indications that Falstaff died repentant; for Theobald's famous emendation "a' babbled of green fields (II.iii.16–17) confirms the impression of a serene death (as Hardin Craig notes: "Falstaff would seem to have been reciting the Twenty-third Psalm"). Henry's repudiation of Falstaff thus appears in the harshest light in *Henry V*; Falstaff's venality appears almost innocent in comparison with the fatal depravity, directly murderous treasons, and wholesale destruction that characterize the latest play in the series. And, while Henry has cast off the person and the outward vices of Falstaff, he has preserved that virtuosity of mind that Falstaff had devoted to the amusement of his friends, but which the king now devotes with terrifying efficiency to coldly political ends, in which it verges on equivocation—if not downright deceit and hypocrisy.

For it is not accidental that the theme of clothes disguising the inner personality (which so characterizes *Mac-*

beth) is strongly stressed in *Henry V*. This motif is not limited to the literal sense involved in the encounter between the disguised king and the blunt soldier Williams, although this ends severely enough in something like a reproach from the commoner:

> Your majesty came not like yourself: you appeared to me but as a common man; witness the night, your garments, your lowliness: and what your highness suffered under that shape, I beseech you take it for your own fault and not mine.
>
> (IV.viii.53–8)

This episode provides an unmistakable analogy to the disguises that had been affected by Henry in order to tease Falstaff in the two preceding plays, although its immediate results are much more serious in the issues raised by the debate with Williams about private responsibility in wartime. However, the theme of disguise is far more uniformly focused on the king than this single episode might suggest. The allusions to his moral transformation are numerous. Even the French Constable cautions the Dauphin against making the kind of misjudgment that Vernon had once warned Hotspur of:

> You shall find his vanities forespent
> Were but the outside of the Roman Brutus
> Covering discretion with a coat of folly.
> (II.iv.36–8)

The opening scene of the play, of course, offers the most sententious recognition of the deceptive capacities of the new king, in the conversation between the two bishops:

> The strawberry grows underneath the nettle
> And wholesome berries thrive and ripen best
> Neighbour'd by fruit of baser quality:
> And so the prince obscured his contemplation
> Under the veil of wildness; which, no doubt,
> Grew like the summer grass, fastest by night,
> Unseen, yet crescive in his faculty.
> (I.i.60–6)

The king is thus established from the start of the play as an elusive personality whose nature has defied prediction. Nor is there any reason to think that, with the assumption of regal dignity, he has also sacrificed the capacity for psychological disguise, any more than he has given up the physical deceptions under the cover of which he continues to explore the minds of his compatriots even after his accession.

Perhaps the most frightening illustration of Henry's mastery of psychological deception appears in his handling of the conspiracy to assassinate him. The evil nature of the intended crime of which the three treacherous English nobles have been accused has been carefully presented so as to justify any handling of their case, yet the fact remains that Henry chooses to play cat and mouse with them. He betrays them into unconsciously sentencing themselves mercilessly, by presenting them with the case of a slight misdemeanor committed against his dignity, which he is choosing to forgive. When they protest that in such cases mercy is unwise, he springs his trap on them and condemns them to death out of their own mouths:

> The mercy that was quick in us but late,
> By your own counsel is suppress'd and kill'd.
>
> (II.ii.79–80)

Later in the play, and much more jestingly, the king is also to lay a little trap for the volatile and self-assured Welshman Fluellen, who will be tricked into a quarrel with Williams; but there the idea is essentially merciful— to save Williams from the dangerous act of striking the king, if he holds to his word and attacks the wearer of the king's favor.

In the case of the three traitors, the issue evolves far more significantly in ways that impugn the character of the king himself, who unconsciously traps himself by his speeches just as had the conspirators. For in his overlong and sententious diatribe against them, Henry marvels at the discrepancy between their conspicuous outward excellence and their unintelligible inward corruption:

Such and so finely bolted didst thou seem:
And thus thy fall hath left a kind of blot,
To mark the full-fraught man and best indued
With some suspicion. I will weep for thee;
For this revolt of thine, methinks, is like
Another fall of man.
　　　(II.ii.137-42)

If one must thus necessarily regard even the "best indued with some suspicion," then Henry himself must be included in our doubtful scrutiny; and of course his allusion to Adam's fall, and the consequent doctrine of all men's involvement in this original sin, *requires* that Henry be recognized as no more infallible than other examples of English nobility. If Shakespeare regards Henry V as the ideal king, it is clearly not in such pagan epic terms as those that have been favored by his critics: the ruthless conquering hero whom the gods uniformly favor.

It is true that, before Harfleur, Henry sounds like Marlowe's Tamburlaine, utterly callous toward those who persist in opposing him:

If I begin the battery once again,
I will not leave the half-achieved Harfleur
Till in her ashes she lie buried.
The gates of mercy shall be all shut up,
And the flesh'd soldier, rough and hard of heart,
In liberty of bloody hand shall range
With conscience wide as hell, mowing like grass
Your fresh-fair virgins and your flowering infants.
　　　(III.iii.6-14)

This hardly sounds like the Christian king which Henry rather too conscientiously insists that he is at other points in the play. He is probably once again affecting an attitude that he does not really accept, in order to attain by psychological means what he has failed to achieve by physical ones. For even his famous speech inciting his troops to return to the siege: "Once more unto the breach, dear friends . . ." (III.i.1ff.) has already *failed* to carry his army to victory by mere force of arms. In fact, that very speech had been followed by a parody of it in the low-life terms of Bardolph and his companions (III.ii.1ff.), and the same scene continues with an embittered debate between the experienced Scottish and Welsh captains about the inadequacy of the siege.

Not only is Henry's army on the verge of disintegration at its first moment of trial, but the king cannot afford to make of Harfleur the bloody example he threatens, because he can hardly hope to avoid the disastrous political consequences that would follow, along the lines of the last phases of the career of his great-uncle, the Black Prince, who had captured and devastated the rebel city of Limoges, only to be forced to abandon all his French possessions subsequently, in part, presumably, because of the indignation and heightened French resistance that resulted. How acutely conscious Henry finally becomes of the need for an intended King of France to handle his future subjects gently appears in his acceptance of the death sentence imposed on Bardolph because, in violation of the army's standing orders, "he hath stolen a pax" (III.vi.42). The theft of even such a small piece of church plate seems to Henry to risk the success of the expedition, and he stresses the care to be taken in preserving French goodwill:

> We would have all such offenders so cut off; and we give express charge, that in our marches through the country, there be nothing compelled from the villages, nothing taken but paid for, none of the French upbraided or abused in disdainful language; for when lenity and cruelty play for kingdom, the gentler gamester is the soonest winner.

> (III.vi.112–20)

Thus Henry's rhetorical performance before the unconquered Harfleur is likely to be nothing more than another stroke of calculated policy. Yet even this is not the reason for Harfleur's surrender, which results simply from its having received news from the Dauphin that he cannot raise an army to relieve it (III.iii.44–50). Neither Henry's bravery nor his rhetoric is therefore the immediate cause of the town's surrender, and it is a chastened Henry who graciously accepts it:

> Open your gates. Come, uncle Exeter,
> Go you and enter Harfleur; there remain,
> And fortify it strongly 'gainst the French:
> Use mercy to them all. For us, dear uncle,
> The winter coming on and sickness growing
> Upon our soldiers, we will retire to Calais.
>
> (III.iii.51–8)

The expedition has proven to be a success, but a precarious one from the very start; its ill-omened conspiracy had shown how necessary the distraction of foreign war still is for the preservation of Henry's authority in England.

In some ways, Henry is thus as guilty of "stealing the pax" as Bardolph—in so far as he has "broken the peace" for his own advantage. That Shakespeare consciously sought the punning analogy may appear from his substitution of "pax" (a plate stamped with Christ's picture) for Holinshed's "pyx" (the vessel containing the consecrated wafer). Whatever the reason for the change, Henry is disadvantaged by it, because his severity toward Bardolph would have been much more justified if the theft had involved sacrilege, as Holinshed's account has it. The kind of counterpoint between the low-life scenes and the major action that we saw in *Henry IV* thus continues in *Henry V*, and we should not assume the irrelevance of such figures as Pistol because they seem so much coarser than Falstaff. Often the words of Bardolph and Pistol anticipate or caricature the nobler strains of Henry himself. We have already seen how Bardolph parodies Henry's futile invocation to renew the assault on Harfleur. Even before the expedition leaves England, Pistol (a low-life caricature of aristocratic bellicosity and sententiousness) has already given his version of the famous St. Crispin's Day speech:

> A noble shalt thou have, and present pay;
> And liquor likewise will I give to thee,

And friendship shall combine, and brotherhood:
I'll live by Nym, and Nym shall live by me;
Is not this just? for I shall sutler be
Unto the camp, and profits shall accrue.
Give me thy hand.
  (II.i.112–8)

This sordid fellowship has the same relationship to Henry's aristocratic profiteering as Falstaff's robberies had to the supposedly "honorable" enterprises of Hotspur, which after all had only the dignity of stealing a kingdom instead of a purse. If only it is big enough, a theft seems to legitimize itself publicly, as Henry IV himself had demonstrated; but the personal moral issues remain the same as for Gadshill or Pistol: the exploitation of public issues for private gain, or at best as political expedients.

We cannot regard Henry's expedition against France as the moral equivalent of his father's intended crusade. Henry's "adventure" is obviously identical to that speciously justified invasion of England by the French in King John's time; for its greedy motives, Arthur's claims had provided a scarcely adequate veil. The Prologue introduced us to Henry V with the assistance of some very dubious terms: if he "assumes the part of Mars," nevertheless:

   . . . at his heels,
Leash'd in like hounds, should famine, sword and fire
Crouch for employment.
  (Prol. 6–8)

Henry is certainly the most powerful personality in this tetralogy, and has most of the attributes of the successful ruler; but if he were always admirable, and never exposed to corrupting situations or learning painful lessons from them, we would have not a play but only the smug epic consecrated to English patriotism that we are sometimes advised to consider the play to be. Only a year or so later Shakespeare will write *Troilus and Cressida*, in which he refuses to treat the Trojan War in epic terms. In it he produces a portrait of the hero Achilles which he refuses to sentimentalize, for he shows us that the hero and the criminal attain their differing ends by a shared contempt for conventional values. The analogy may encourage us to recognize that Henry V is shown to us as a great leader, but not as an infallible one. Shakespeare never violates Christian theology to the point of presenting a portrait of unqualified human virtue in any of his heroes—and if he had attempted to do so, he would surely have falsified the essence of drama: conflict between two roughly equivalent but incompatible forces. Henry has all the defects of a great leader.

One may nevertheless feel inclined to doubt the validity of such a tension on any large scale in *Henry V*. The English seem to be too strongly favored, and their French opponents too contemptible for that. Yet we must recognize the recurrent polarity in the tetralogy between the idealizing romantic temperament on the one hand, and that of the narrowly political manipulator on the other. Richard II surrenders his picturesque but erratic government to Bolingbroke, whose chill and monochromatic rule antagonizes such romantic rebels as Hotspur. When Henry V inherits a pacified kingdom, he directs it by exploiting the traditional Lancastrian potentialities against the national entity that shares the archaic values of such figures as Richard and Hotspur: the high culture of medieval France. For all his sophistication as a politician, Henry knows that he is almost a barbarian in the eyes of the sophisticated French court: hence the affected bluntness of his courtship of Katharine. Henry and his followers thus stand in the same relationship to the French as the cunning and intellectual Greeks do to the witty and gallant Trojans in *Troilus and Cressida* (of which Shakespeare is perhaps already thinking, as Pistol's first quoted speech has shown us). But are the forces and associations of England and France sufficiently balanced to suggest a truly creative conflict in the Hegelian manner, so that the climactic marriage acquires symbolic overtones?

We must first consider the presentation of the situation in the opening scenes of *Henry V*. It is not enough simply to impose our knowledge of Henry IV's cunning advice to his son, in the earlier play, to pursue "foreign quarrels" (*2HIV*, IV.v.215), on the pious figure that the new king presents in the opening scenes of *Henry V*. For any interpretation to carry conviction, the play must make its point in its own terms. However, its opening scene does suggest the same political maneuvering as characterized *Henry IV*. In it, the king is praised by the Archbishop of Canterbury for his military and religious insight, but also for his political finesse:

> Turn him to any cause of policy
> The Gordian knot of it he will unloose
> Familiar as his garter.
> (I.i.45–7)

This deftness rapidly appears, for the Church is shown to be a victim of what the modern bridge player calls a "squeeze play." The king has, by calculation, chosen to "seem indifferent" to a bill revived from the previous Parliament, of which the Archbishop of Canterbury says with distress:

> If it pass against us,
> We lose the better half of our possession:
> For all the temporal lands which men devout
> By testament have given to the church
> Would they strip from us.
> (I.i.7–11)

The authority of the king offers the only hope to the ecclesiastics against the will of Parliament, and at the price Henry demands of them they have succeeded in influencing the king's public posture so that he is now

> . . . swaying more upon our part
> Than cherishing the exhibiters against us;
> For I have made an offer to his majesty, . . .
> As touching France, to give a greater sum

> Than ever at one time the clergy yet
> Did to his predecessors part withall.
> (I.i.73–5,79–81)

Henry thus obtains personally (instead of at the discretion of Parliament) the means to finance his French expedition, as well as the ecclesiastical sanctions that had seemed so vital to the mounting of the second rebellion against Henry IV. Parliament's hostility to the Church meanwhile remains a useful lever with which to control the bishops' responses to Henry's later intentions. Thus the long second scene of the play in which the king canvasses opinion about the proposed war with France is no less cunningly stage-managed than is Henry IV's striking opening speech at the start of the first part of *Henry IV*. Henry V complacently lays on the head of the Archbishop of Canterbury the full onus of responsibility for the claim to the French throne, confident that the Church is as anxious as the monarchy "to busy giddy minds with foreign quarrels" (*2HIV*, IV.v.214–15):

> And God forbid, my dear and faithful lord,
> That you should fashion, wrest, or bow your reading,
> Or nicely charge your understanding soul
> With opening titles miscreate, whose right
> Suits not in native colours with the truth;
> For God doth know how many now in health
> Shall drop their blood in approbation
> Of what your reverence shall incite us to.
> Therefore take heed how you impawn our person,
> How you awake our sleeping sword of war:
> We charge you, in the name of God, take heed.
> (I.ii.13–23)

Even to so relentless a transfer of responsibility as this the archbishop feels obliged to offer the fullest acceptance: "The sin upon my head, dread sovereign!" (I.ii.97) Henry thus has the money for his scheme and complete freedom of conscience in pursuing it without the least risk that his ecclesiastical authority will play any such theological tricks on him as Pandulph appeared to play on his French supporters in *King John*.

It now needs only the clumsy provocation of the Dauphin's mocking gift of tennis balls to lend the final edge of "legitimate" resentment to Henry's public intention—but even before the French ambassador's undiplomatic present, Henry has already firmly resolved to overturn the French monarchy:

Call in the messengers sent from the Dauphin.
Now are we well resolved; and, by God's help,
And yours, the noble sinews of our power,
France being ours, we'll bend it to our awe,
Or break it all to pieces: or there we'll sit,
Ruling in large and ample empery
O'er France and all her almost kingly dukedoms,
Or lay these bones in an unworthy urn.
(I.ii.221–8)

Are these really the words of "the ideal king"? "We'll bend it to our awe,/Or break it all in pieces" looks forward by contrast to such tragic figures as Macbeth and Lear. The choice of death or glory subsequently offered in this speech is an echo of Hotspur's suicidal heroism. Henry V is a young man's hero, at this point, rather than an ideal king: Alexander, indeed, rather than Augustus Caesar.

Even the Chorus introduces a hint of irony into his Prologue to Act II as he notes that "all the youth of England are on fire" and "sell the pasture now to buy the horse." There is more than a hint here of proverbial reproach for youthful improvidence, and indeed the major part of Henry's expedition suggests that it is mounted in a state of mind comparable to Hotspur's intoxicated ambition before his dramatic assault on the English throne:

Imagination of some great exploit
Drives him beyond the bounds of patience.
(*1HIV*, I.iii.199–200)

Not only does Henry at the start tend to talk of war with the same cheerful exuberance as if it were a game of tennis ("The game's afoot" [III.i.32]), but his terms to the French king are so outrageous that Hotspur at his wildest would never have dared publicly to propose such demands as Exeter transmits on Henry's behalf:

> When you find him evenly derived
> From his most famed of famous ancestors,
> Edward the Third, he bids you then resign
> Your crown and kingdom, indirectly held
> From him the native and true challenger.
>   (II.iv.91–5)

It is not credible that Shakespeare should have forgotten the analogy to this fantastic proposition that he had presented earlier, in the French king's expectation in *King John* that England would be surrendered to him by John merely because he urged the superior legal title of his juvenile protégé Arthur. And when Exeter urges the French king nobly to surrender because of the suffering that resistance would produce, one feels that the plea is a rather paradoxical one for an aggressor to make. It is no more significant than Henry's fierce threats to Harfleur.

Henry thus appears not as the ideal ruler, but as the youthful hero, already tempered by a broader range of experience than Hotspur's, but still drawn (despite ulterior political motives) to the same dashing, risky, and destructive enterprises as his erstwhile enemy. The English cannot therefore be accurately seen by Shakespeare's audience as merely idealized compatriots. Even Henry in his speech before Harfleur recognizes that his army is full of men like Bardolph and Pistol, rather than romantic heroes like Suffolk and York (who die so picturesquely at Agincourt, IV.v.):

> What rein can hold licentious wickedness
> When down the hill he holds his fierce career?
> We may as bootless spend our vain command
> Upon the enraged soldiers in their spoil

As send precepts to the Leviathan
To come ashore.
(III.iii.22–7)

This pattern of analogy may well have suggested the title
for Hobbes' study of the untamable viciousness of men
once they are freed from strict discipline. Henry has
turned on France those forces that he feared at home in
England; but in the beginning he rides the crest of the
rapidly breaking wave of the English invasion with a delight that is scarcely compatible with the issues involved—
just as Antony is to gloat over the prospect of firing the
civil wars in Rome through which Caesar's murder will be
avenged, in *Julius Caesar* (III.ii.265–6). Both men are to
pay a price for their satisfaction in the role of manipulator
of human passions: Antony's will be his own destruction,
Henry's the happier one of the sacrifice of his bellicose
exuberance for a more sober humility. For it must be recognized that the first phase of Henry's reign displays a
smug self-confidence which, while never making him as
politically insensitive as Richard II first appears to be, is
nevertheless closer to the headstrong spirit of Roland
which leads to the tragic disaster at Roncesvalles, than to
the serene wisdom of Charlemagne, in the *Chanson de
Roland*.

Henry has to learn moderation; his firm denunciation
of Bardolph's minor theft in Act III, Scene vi, suggests
how cautious he has become in the later phases of his
campaign: "when lenity and cruelty play for a kingdom,
the gentler gamester is the soonest winner" (III.vi.120).
At this point the king has all but abandoned his hopes for
the present expedition, which Shakespeare has shown us
to be dignified alone by the isolated and insignificant surrender of Harfleur. Thus, when the French herald brings
Henry news of the French intention to challenge his passage (in a speech full of the same bravado that had initially been cause for affront, in the presentation of the
tennis balls), Henry is now willing to buckle down his

pride and to ask with moderation for the opportunity to pass peacefully home to England:

> Thou dost thy office fairly. Turn thee back,
> And tell thy king I do not seek him now;
> But would be willing to march on to Calais
> Without impeachment: for to say the sooth,
> Though 'tis no wisdom to confess so much
> Unto an enemy of craft and vantage,
> My people are with sickness much enfeebled,
> My numbers lessened, and those few I have
> Almost no better than so many French.
> (III.vi.148–56)

It is to this low pitch that the original wild hopes of the English invaders have been reduced; instead of:

> . . . crowns imperial, crowns and coronets,
> Promised to Harry and his followers
> (II.Prol. 10–11)

there is left only the rueful recognition for Henry that:

> My ransom is this frail and worthless trunk,
> My army but a weak and sickly guard.
> (III.vi.163–4)

The epic tone and the ruthless political finesse have been replaced by a new simplicity and candor. The threat of failure has increased Henry's stature as a man, even if he sounds less dazzling as a leader. He has learnt the bitter lesson of the need for moderation in one's demands which fate lays upon the invader of foreign soil, at least in the plays of Shakespeare. His retreat is indeed determined more by such hostile "acts of God" as sickness and disease than by the effective opposition of the French who, with unconscious wisdom, have played a waiting game.

It is at this point that a truer balance can be struck between the opposing forces. Henry's invasion of France may have been politically expedient domestically, but it was mounted in a spirit of brash confidence and chauvinistic indifference for the well-being of his intended kingdom. This well-being he has now come to respect, having found it impossible to maintain himself in France merely by armed might. The French inertia has thus already effectively defeated the hubristic energy of the invaders, rather as Tolstoy later shows us in *War and Peace* how the vastness of Russia swallows up Napoleon's Grand Army, without ever directly confronting it in decisive battle. But if the French are now effectively masters of the situation, the question remains whether they will ultimately handle this advantage wisely. The humiliation of invasion has increasingly made the discreet policy of the French king intolerable to such bellicose spirits as the Dauphin's. Thus, at the very moment when France, as "the gentler gamester," is winning the match, this policy is overthrown in favor of a more flamboyant one, aimed less at the expulsion of the English than at their total annihilation, which is gloatingly anticipated in a spirit no less hubristic than that of the original English enthusiasm for the invasion:

> Do but behold yon poor and starved band,
> And your fair show shall suck away their souls,
> Leaving them but the shales and husks of men.
> There is not work enough for all our hands;
> Scarce blood enough in all their sickly veins
> To give each naked curtle-axe a stain,
> That our French gallants shall today draw out,
> And sheathe for lack of sport: let us but blow on them,
> The vapour of our valour will o'erturn them.
> 'Tis positive 'gainst all exceptions, lords,
> That our superfluous lackeys and our peasants,
> Who in unnecessary action swarm
> About our squares of battle, were enow
> To purge this field of such a hilding foe,
> Though we upon this mountain's basis by
> Took stand for idle speculation.
>
> (IV.ii.16–31)

The chivalric insolence of this speech provides us with both an echo of the earlier Henry V, and a contrast with his more recent frame of mind.

The center of the play lies in the scene (IV.i.) in which Henry V and his army review their fate soberly, man to man, without the intrusion of any of that aristocratic contempt for the common foot-soldier that is so marked in the speech of the Constable of France just noted. Indeed, Shakespeare cleverly uses the theme of Shylock's famous demonstration of the humanity of the despised Jewish race to demonstrate the equally mundane nature of kings, for Henry has been made to recognize that he has no more deserved unusual favor as a king than has the most wretched of his subjects:

> I think the king is but a man, as I am: the violet smells to him as it doth to me; the element shows to him as it does to me; all his senses have but human conditions: his ceremonies laid by, in his nakedness he appears but a man; and though his affections are higher mounted than ours, yet, when they stoop, they stoop with the like wing.

(IV.i.104–10)

It is no accident that it is precisely the lack of this knowledge of oneself to which Henry has attained that later provokes Lear's tragic misunderstanding of *his* kingly role; and its attainment through far more intense effort than Henry's constitutes the essential content of Lear's suffering in the storm. Williams' assumption that the king is wholly responsible for his followers' misfortunes (IV.i.140ff.) adds a further disturbing consideration to Henry's anxieties. He answers bravely for himself, concealed by his disguise, maintaining that, "his cause being just and his quarrel honorable" (as the Archbishop had guaranteed), then "the king is not bound to answer the particular endings of his soldiers, the father of his son, nor the master of his servants; for they purpose not their death, when they purpose their services" (IV.i.162–5).

The king refuses responsibility for the spiritual condition of those who die in sin as a result of his orders, plausibly affirming that the proper regulation of their minds is as much their responsibility as their obligation to serve is the right of the just king: "Every subject's duty is the king's; but every subject's soul is his own" (IV.i.187–8). Again the recognition is an anticipation of Hobbes' insistence that the state's authority may not be publicly questioned, although a man's most private thoughts properly lie outside the scope of public concern. Henry thus painfully, and under acute personal and public pressure, labors toward a code of public and private responsibility. It is perhaps an unfashionable code nowadays intellectually; but the basis for all law and order still lies in respect for legally established practice, and Shakespeare will duly show in *Julius Caesar* (as Hobbes will also declare) that, once complete freedom of conscience and of consequent action is assumed, murderous anarchy alone can immediately result, with the ultimate establishment of absolute tyranny as the only defense against individual men's assertion of endlessly conflicting aspirations.

At his moment of most intense political awareness, Henry V thus comes to conclusions that wholly destroy any justifications for those actions of his father to which Henry V ultimately owes his crown. The scene must inevitably end with Henry's recognition of this bitter truth:

> Not today, O Lord,
> O, not today, think not upon the fault
> My father made in compassing the crown!
> I Richard's body have interred new;
> And on it have bestow'd more contrite tears
> Than from it issued forced drops of blood: . . .
> Though all that I can do is nothing worth,
> Since that my penitence comes after all,
> Imploring pardon.
> (IV.i.308–13,320–3)

All that he had welcomed on his accession to the throne has thus been drastically impaired; his title and his authority dwindle to the sacrifice of private personality to public needs:

> What infinite heart's ease
> Must kings neglect, that private men enjoy!

And what have kings, that privates have not too,
Save ceremony, save general ceremony?
(IV.i.253-6)

However, even at this moment of truth, Shakespeare characteristically does not hesitate to add a dash of irony in Henry's somewhat inappropriate reflection on the rigors of that "watch the king keeps to maintain the peace" (IV.i.300). Up to this point, Henry has certainly *not* "watched" enough to seek the means to peace—rather the reverse, though from this point on in the play he will not fail to seek it by all means, fighting only when battle is forced on him.

The logic of the French defeat at Agincourt is thus, from Shakespeare's point of view, fully apparent. While Henry now recognizes the nature of his office and tries to come to terms with his peril and his conscience, the French loudly celebrate their anticipated victory, dissipating their energies and giving offense to the sober Welsh captain, Fluellen, who insists that the English keep their ancient discipline, to Henry's satisfaction:

Though it appear a little out of fashion
There is much care and valour in this Welshman.
(IV.i.84-5)

The French meantime quarrel and exchange vainglorious epigrams, ridiculing their opponents: "If the English had any apprehension, they would run away" (III.vii.145-6). It is now very much a confrontation such as we saw in the first part of *Henry IV*: on the one hand the arbitrary charm and chivalry of a Hotspur, on the other the shambling forces deployed by Henry IV in the service of vestigial law and order. At Agincourt, the English look as unprepossessing as Falstaff's ragged regiment, as Grandpré declares:

Why do you stay so long, my lords of France?
Yon island carrions, desperate of their bones,
Ill-favouredly become the morning field:
Their ragged curtains poorly are let loose,

And our air shakes them passing scornfully: . . .
Description cannot suit itself in words
To demonstrate the life of such a battle
In life so lifeless as it shows itself.
                    (IV.ii.38–42,53–5)

The fact nevertheless remains that this battered army is
out in due order on the battlefield long before the French
—as the Constable says: "They have said their prayers,
and they stay for death" (IV.ii.56). Wisdom now rides
with the English, as earlier it had ridden with the French
king. Henry has shown to the full that power to fuse the
loyalties of all the classes of English society that he had
derived long before from drinking with the tapsters in
Eastcheap. His troops may be ragged, but they are bound
to him by a bond of community that his last speech to
them on St. Crispin's Day has shown him to be able to
draw to the tightest:

And Crispin Crispian shall ne'er go by,
From this day to the ending of the world,
But we in it shall be remembered;
We few, we happy few, we band of brothers;
For he today that sheds his blood with me
Shall be my brother; be he ne'er so vile,
This day shall gentle his condition.
                    (IV.iii.57–63)

At this point, Henry's rhetoric touches true nobility,
affirming his reaccepance of his erstwhile low-life companions on fair terms and expiating his cruelty to Falstaff.
This markedly contrasts with the superciliousness of the
aristocratic French and with their complacent assumption
of victory, which fully justifies Henry's contemptuous
allusion to the old fable:

The man that once did sell the lion's skin
While the beast lived, was killed with hunting him.
                    (IV.iii.93–4)

The English victory becomes fully intelligible in this
moral context—yet we must beware of simplifying its

nature. The battle moves forward to a conclusion in which both sides are guilty of barbarities: the French murder the English boys, the English their French prisoners. Henry himself is censured by Williams for spying on his men in the guise of a private gentleman on the eve of the battle. Such darker notes tone down the splendor of the victory and legitimize the temperate response of Henry to the low English casualty list, which he discreetly ascribes to the Providence of God (as the Elizabethans did with the defeat of the Armada):

> O God, thy arm was here;
> And not to us, but to thy arm alone,
> Ascribe we all! When without stratagem,
> But in plain shock and even play of battle,
> Was ever known so great and little loss
> On one part and on the other? Take it, God,
> For it is none but thine.
> (IV.viii.111-17)

Henry thus finally discards the heroic role which, at the start of the expedition, he had seemed to inherit from Hotspur. The subsequent humiliation of Pistol, the corrupt military "humor," symbolically completes the deflation of bellicosity, whose horrors are depicted by the Duke of Burgundy, when he declares that Peace

> . . . hath from France too long been chased,
> And all her husbandry doth lie on heaps
> Corrupting in its own fertility. . . .
> And as our vineyards, fallows, meads and hedges,
> Defective in their natures, grow to wildness,
> Even so our houses and ourselves and children
> Have lost, or do not learn for want of time,
> The sciences that should become our country;
> But grow like savages,—as soldiers will
> That nothing do but meditate on blood,—
> To swearing and stern looks, defused attire
> And every thing that seems unnatural.
> (V.ii.38-40,54-62)

It is to this condition that Henry's earlier relentless pursuit of a supposedly legal title has reduced the goal of his efforts.

In his pressing of the negotiations for peace, however, one feels a new gentleness and consideration in Henry's bearing. Thus the rigor of his terms is softened by his words to the French queen about her daughter:

> Yet leave our cousin Katharine here with us:
> She is our capital demand, comprised
> Within the fore-rank of our articles.
>   (V.ii.95-7)

At first, his courtship follows very much the pattern of bluntness that Burgundy had censured as the symptom of too much soldiering. However, we may recall how badly affectation of speech and manner served the cause of the aristocratic suitors in *Love's Labour's Lost*, and how attractive Hotspur's good-humored teasing of an earlier Kate had appeared in the first part of *Henry IV*. The later Henry's poise and good sense cut even more impressively through the overrefined manners of the French court than his sword once did through their army:

> O Kate, nice customs curtsy to great kings. Dear Kate, you and I cannot be confined within the weak list of a country's fashion: we are the makers of manners, Kate; and the liberty that follows our places stops the mouth of all find-faults; as I will do yours, for upholding the nice fashion of your country in denying me a kiss.
>   (V.ii.293-9)

This is a more gracious and a more happily rewarded encounter than that on the battlefield, for Henry is the gainer by it, even though he drily observes:

> You may, some of you, thank love for my blindness, who cannot see many a fair French city for one fair French maid that stands in my way.
>   (V.ii.343-6)

Still the French king announces that "We have consented to all terms of reason" (V.ii.358). Henry abandons his extravagant claim to immediate succession to the French throne in favor of a diplomatic formula that promises his ultimate succession (a formula, incidentally, that is to lead to those disastrous wars during the reign of his juvenile and incompetent son and successor that were treated at length in *Henry VI*). Henry's title to both thrones is thus reinforced, without resort to extreme measures. Indeed, as the Chorus' last speech recognizes, it is ultimately less his unassisted merits that have won Henry victory than Providence:

> Fortune made his sword;
> By which the world's best garden he achieved,
> And of it left his son imperial lord.
> (Epil. 6–8)

The echo of Burgundy's plea for the arts of peace is unmistakable—just as unmistakable as the bitter moral of the succeeding references to the renewed collapse of this new order into a new chaos under Henry VI. All that will really be left is the lesson of the success of Henry V, which is based not on the romantic bellicosity of a clever young hero masquerading as the ideal king, but on the ultimate steadiness attained by a mature man who knows his failures and, regretting them, puts his trust in Providence. If Henry were held to be a perfect ruler from the start of his reign, this maturation could scarcely be recognized, and the play would lack that central purpose that lends each Shakespearean drama its subtle integrity and evolution.

IV

THE ROMAN PLAYS

I

⌘ *Julius Caesar*

IN *Julius Caesar*, Shakespeare carries his investigation of the dynamics of the political activity one stage further. His choice of Roman society as the illustration for this development was partly in response to the current humanist interest in the classics, but it was also a safeguard against the risk of impolitic contemporary applications, such as could be derived, to his danger, even from his portrayal of so remote a reign as that of Richard II. Pagan society, unpossessed by the acute sense of hierarchy that governed men's minds during the Middle Ages and the Renaissance, displayed in its most spontaneous form those rhythms of political succession that fascinated Shakespeare. In *Julius Caesar* he constructed a play that defied all conventional modes of dramatic unity, in order to embrace the greatest possible number of revolutions of the wheel of political fortune. Pompey's defeat and death are the theme of the opening scene; Caesar's assassination occupies the earlier acts; the defeat of Brutus and Cassius is the concern of the later ones; the conclusion marks the temporary supremacy of Antony, which we may already discern falling under the threat of Octavius.

In an attempt to simplify this structure, Shakespeare's play has been described as the tragedy of Brutus, but this is just as much a distortion as to interpret *Richard II* as the tragedy of its nominally central figure. In both cases, the political pattern that is subtly evoked transcends in interest the vicissitudes of any single character. This explains the curious handling of Caesar's career, which cannot usually provide a unifying concern for a critic of this play except by such ingenious arguments as the suggestion that the second half of the play constitutes Caesar's revenge—although in it Caesar functions as a political force only through Antony's rhetoric. The apparition that appears to Brutus before Philippi obviously has no moral, political, or even psychological authority, since Brutus has only to reassert his self-confidence for it to vanish, without leaving any of that metaphysical aura so marked in the last dream of Richard III. The world of the classical history play has few of the medieval attributes of such English tyrants as Richard III: men's acts seem to be related only to those sanctions that they choose to invite, not to any providential order. Antony may act as ruthlessly as Richard III, but the play suggests that he need fear no penalties for his amorality, as long as his nerves and his political judgment do not weaken.

It is precisely the purely personal slackening of political acumen that Shakespeare has striven to evoke in his aging Julius Caesar—a portrait of decline drawn at the expense of strict fidelity to North's translation of Plutarch, on which the dramatist depended for most of his details. Caesar is the first of those aging yet still monumental figures, cast in the mold of Sophocles' Oedipus, that preside over many of Shakespeare's mature tragedies: Othello, Lear, Antony. This study shows what happens to a Henry V if he grows old in triumph without perpetually relearning the lesson he so painfully learned before Agincourt. There is still no question, however, of the superiority of Caesar's political instincts to those of all the men around him. His insight into his most dangerous opponent, Cassius, is limited only by the complacent assurance that he no longer needs to act on such judgments:

> . . . if my name were liable to fear,
> I do not know the man I should avoid
> So soon as that spare Cassius. He reads much;
> He is a great observer and he looks

Quite through the deeds of men; . . .
Such men as he be never at heart's ease
Whiles they behold a greater than themselves,
And therefore are they very dangerous.
I rather tell thee what is to be fear'd
Than what I fear; for always I am Caesar.
Come on my right hand, for this ear is deaf,
And tell me truly what thou think'st of him.
(I.ii.199–203,208–14)

There is an economical boldness in the characterization
of decaying genius in this speech. Shakespeare stresses the
strength of Caesar's insight by setting the passage immediately after Cassius has provocatively vented his resentment
at Caesar's power, in his conversation with Brutus:

Why, man, he doth bestride the narrow world
Like a Colossus, and we petty men
Walk under his huge legs and peep about
To find ourselves dishonourable graves.
(I.ii.135–8)

While Caesar evaluates Cassius with precision, he shows indifference to those immediate advantages that are to be
gained by applying such insights to practical purposes (as
Cassius does with Brutus) a sign of petrifying political
judgment. Caesar's ultimate triumph is shown by Shakespeare to have been accompanied by a decline in flexibility,
which is almost always fatal to a politician. Caesar cannot
afford not to fear, and the decay of judgment that is
implicit in his neglect of such inward perceptions is subtly
reinforced by the symptoms of decline in his outward
ones, such as his partial deafness (I.ii.213).

There is a subtle augury in the bearing that this loss of
effectiveness has on our sense of Caesar's omnipotence,
since his dangerous self-assurance echoes that very com-
placency that is a familiar theme in the censure of Richard
II. Caesar feels that his superiority verges on the transcendent; his profound preoccupation with the kingship
proffered by Antony suggests how closely he approaches
the medieval role of the English kings in Shakespeare's

plays. His physical collapse at the climax of this public invitation to accept absolute power reflects the very intensity of this concern and at the same time, once again, the failure of efficiency in a man past his prime, who is no longer able to take decisive action.

However, Shakespeare does not seek simply to document more severely than does Plutarch the last erratic phases of a masterly public career. He is concerned to postulate the gravest kind of challenge to accepted order: the surrender of traditional institutions to the whims of an increasingly unreliable yet unrelentingly self-confident tyrant. Of the disastrous future of a Rome under Caesar, Shakespeare leaves us in little doubt just before the assassination, when Caesar appears in the full flow of monarchical absolutism:

> I could be well moved, if I were as you;
> If I could pray to move, prayers would move me:
> But I am constant as the northern star,
> Of whose true-fix'd and resting quality
> There is no fellow in the firmament. . . .
> So in the world; 'tis furnish'd well with men,
> And men are flesh and blood, and apprehensive;
> Yet in the number I do know but one
> That unassailable holds on his rank
> Unshaked of motion: and that I am he, . . .
>   (III.i.58–62,66–70)

The vulgar self-deception that is involved in the smug assumption of this role of demigod is dramatized by the way in which Caesar's self-asserted steadfastness appears as a contrast with his pathetic vacillations—a mere hundred lines or so earlier in the play—about whether or not to go to the capitol. One regrets the loss of the original version of another of these assertions made by Caesar just before his death, which now reads: "Caesar doth not wrong, nor without cause / Will he be satisfied" (III.i.47–8)—a flat statement, which Jonson's ridicule supposedly encouraged Shakespeare to substitute for the original megalomaniac *non sequitur*: "Caesar did never wrong but with just cause." This original reading suggests how dangerous a ruler the increasingly lunatic egotism of Julius Caesar would be bound to make him, if his advance to absolute supremacy were to be completed.

The situation is carefully mounted (even at the expense of some supposed distortion of history) so as to lend credence to the reasoning that governs Brutus' famous homicidal soliloquy at the start of Act II, which begins with the crucial decision: "It must be by his death" (II.i.10), and then proceeds to pile up hypotheses with which to justify the assassination that has already been decided on. Though Brutus can find "no personal cause" to resent Caesar (unlike Cassius), he finds the "general" argument against monarchy irresistible because, despite Caesar's apparent decorum, monarchy leads naturally to the establishment of tyranny:

> So Caesar may,
> Then, lest he may, prevent. And since the quarrel
> Will bear no colour for the thing he is,
> Fashion it thus; that what he is, augmented,
> Would run to these and these extremities:
> And therefore think him as a serpent's egg
> Which, hatch'd, would as his kind, grow mischievous,
> And kill him in the shell.
> (II.i.27–34)

The ironies and inadequacies of this analysis are manifold. Brutus, the conscientious political philosopher, is apparently utterly unconscious of the arbitrary (not to say inverted) nature of his logic, whose ultimate justification is an assertion that is at best hypothetical: "So Caesar may." No system of justice has ever yet succeeded in effectively evaluating criminal intent—particularly when, as in this case, the prosecutor cannot even bring in circumstantial evidence, because he still lacks the perception to recognize that his own hypothesis of Caesar's manic tyranny has already been realized in all but title.

Not only is Brutus illogical and politically naive, he is also unaware of his own motivations, and of those of the other elements of Roman society with which he is familiar.

Nevertheless, through his simple sincerity he exercises a magnetism over those who know him well, as we see in the reaction of the sick Ligarius, who responds enthusiastically to his mere presence:

> Set on your foot,
> And with a heart new-fired I follow you,
> To do I know not what: but it sufficeth
> That Brutus leads me on.
> (II.i.331-4)

Such hypnotic integrity confirms the fact that we have in Brutus an archetypal example of the extraordinary power of utter sincerity, a power that Cassius wisely plots to exploit in the interest of the assassination, as Casca recognizes:

> O, he sits high in all the people's hearts:
> And that which would appear offence in us,
> His countenance, like richest alchemy,
> Will change to virtue and to worthiness.
> (I.iii.157-60)

At this point, the bearing of this Roman play on the second tetralogy of English history plays begins to become visible. Henry V had exclaimed to Lord Scoop, his intended assassin:

> . . . thou, 'gainst all proportion, didst bring in
> Wonder to wait on treason and on murder.
> (HV, II.ii.109-10)

While Henry is baffled to understand the motivations behind such a conspiracy, *Julius Caesar* presents it, as it were, from the inside; we find that assassins may well be made of the most conventionally admirable men, and precisely because of their innocence. The role of Brutus is not unlike that of the Archbishop of York in the second part of *Henry IV*, whose unconscious sophistries provide a screen of moralizing behind which is concealed what is essentially a final blow to the precarious stability of the body politic. In fact, the situation at the start of the two plays is surprisingly similar. After the wars between Pompey and Caesar (which ended in the assassination of the former, in circumstances analogous to the death of Richard II), Roman institutions were shaken to the core, just as Bolingbroke's deposition of Richard had invalidated the premises of medieval monarchy.

The further major distortions of public values that are implicit in the assassinations are reflected in the progressive disintegration of the norms of social conduct throughout the two societies. Plato's pessimistic cycle of aristocracy, oligarchy, democracy, and tyranny is well launched toward its third phase of mob-rule in the Rome of the opening scene of *Julius Caesar*. The tribunes reproach the people for their incipient anarchy, and attempt to arrest the inevitable symptoms of the approaching tyranny of the Caesars. In the second scene of the play, however, the impossibility of arresting the relentless cycle appears in the dry comment of Casca that the tribunes, "for pulling scarfs off Caesar's images, are put to silence" (I.ii.289–90). Brutus' political program thus has an element of absurdity from the start; the question is not "Can the Republic be saved from tyranny?" but "Which tyrant is to be preferred?" This is made repeatedly obvious throughout the play, most ironically perhaps at the point when the populace, excited by Brutus' appearance of authority in the meeting after the assassination, seems willing to make Brutus himself its new monarch: "Let him be Caesar," and proposes to this newest murderer the same triumphal procession that had previously been given to the murderer of Pompey: Caesar himself.

Brutus is incapable, however, of recognizing this volatile, indeed nihilistic condition of men who have been freed from conventional social restraints—a condition that Shakespeare deliberately dramatizes by introducing the scene in which the mob murders Cinna the poet, merely because he happens to have the same name as one of the conspirators. This scene is a Hobbesian vision of human depravity, if ever there was one; it is not surprising that, in the face of this violence, so calculatingly set in motion by Antony,

> Brutus and Cassius
> Are rid like madmen through the gates of Rome.
> (III.ii.273-4)

Up to this point Brutus has obviously no sense of the forces that have been latent in Rome from the start of the play; he cannot conceive of the explosions that will result from tampering with the precarious equilibrium on purely theoretical grounds. Cassius is more alert to the risks, and more competent in neutralizing them; but there is irony in the fact that his stature is insufficient to sustain his intended public role without the support of Brutus. Once Brutus has become involved, his very useful virtues of integrity disrupt the ruthless efficiency of Cassius' plot, at the same time as their popular appeal makes that plot possible. The relationship between the two characters thus hardly bears out the validity of the philosophic associations with which their roles have been traditionally invested (Brutus as a Stoic, Cassius as an Epicurean). The central pattern has instead the form of the deceiver who is destroyed by his own dupe's naivety.

From the very first encounter between Brutus and Cassius, this harsh rhythm is established. It is heralded chorically by the unintended truth of Caesar's pronouncement on the soothsayer's warning: "He is a dreamer; let us leave him" (I.ii.24). Caesar's judgment happens to be wrong locally, as the fulfillment of the augury demonstrates, but his suspicion of intellectuals and idealists is an omen of Cassius' plight in having to depend on Brutus' power to rationalize his every act. Brutus believes in the adequacy of private human judgment to meet any demands that are made on it, by both public and private affairs, with the result that he is perpetually given to merely logical arguments for courses of conduct that violate the rhythms of experience. Again and again, Brutus reasons himself into acts that are at odds with good sense, as Cassius is prompt to note:

> Well, Brutus, thou art noble; yet, I see,
> Thy honorable metal may be wrought
> From that it is disposed: therefore it is meet
> That noble minds keep ever with their likes;
> For who so firm that cannot be seduced?
> Caesar doth bear me hard; but he loves Brutus:
> If I were Brutus now and he were Cassius,
> He should not humour me.
>   (I.ii.312–19)

It is Cassius rather than Brutus, however, who demands the most serious political consideration, even though it is Brutus throughout whose blunders precipitate disaster. There is a ruthless precision about Cassius that suggests that he is indeed potentially Caesar's successor. While Brutus is fussing about such tangential issues as whether or not the conspirators should take an oath, Cassius is perpetually preparing for significant contingencies that may effect the ultimate results of the assassination. To an inquiry about further executions, he replies:

> Decius, well urged: I think it is not meet,
> Mark Antony, so well beloved of Caesar,
> Should outlive Caesar: we shall find of him
> A shrewd contriver; and, you know, his means,
> If he improve them, may well stretch so far
> As to annoy us all: which to prevent,
> Let Antony and Caesar fall together.
>   (II.i.155–61)

Events prove that this brutal policy would have been the more expedient, but Brutus is too concerned with the ritual formality of the assassination to want to blemish it by such undignified corollaries of the initial murder. Like Richard II, Brutus continually mistakes a decision for an event, and an act for a fully accomplished policy. Typically, it is he who suggests to the conspirators the visible symbolism of smearing their arms with Caesar's blood, and feels it proper to allow Caesar the formal funeral that gives Antony his chance to sway the mob. Cassius dispenses with such high themes in trying to secure Antony's reconciliation to the conspirators, bluntly proposing far more attractive motives than Brutus' naive ideals:

> Your voice shall be as strong as any man's
> In the disposing of new dignities.
> (III.i.177–8)

Later, in the famous quarrel scene, Cassius is justifiably enraged by the condescending, even pedagogical tone that Brutus assumes in playing the role of the philosopher who is set against the inferior sensibilities of the mere man of affairs. The almost grotesque lack of even a minimum of self-awareness in Brutus appears in the sequel to his censure of Cassius for taking bribes (IV.iii.9–11):

> You have done that you should be sorry for.
> There is no terror, Cassius, in your threats,
> For I am arm'd so strong in honesty
> That they pass by me as the idle wind,
> Which I respect not. I did send to you
> For certain sums of gold, which you denied me:
> For I can raise no money by vile means:
> By heaven, I had rather coin my heart,
> And drop my blood for drachmas, than to wring
> From the hard hands of peasants their vile trash
> By any indirection: I did send
> To you for gold to pay my legions,
> Which you denied me: was that done like Cassius?
> (IV.iii.65–77)

It is a ruthless stroke of characterization to show Brutus at once censuring Cassius for mercenary behavior, praising his own undeviating integrity, and yet complaining that Cassius has not given him a fair share of the tainted gold to meet his needs. Brutus' is clearly a mind not in full possession of itself; it is this that makes it the major cause of the failure of the conspiracy to establish its own hegemony, and the instrument of what in some senses might be held to be the tragedy of Cassius, who is the nearest to being an effective personality.

For there can be no question that Antony is a more erratic and thus a far more terrifying figure than Cassius. Cassius is concerned simply with self-preservation and with the pragmatic means for securing this understandable goal. In Antony, however, there is a kind of inspired nihilism, which is perfectly in tune with the moods of the mob. One can see how utterly alienated he must feel from virtue of the naive and yet bloody character that is favored by Brutus; the consequences of this alienation prove to be the total disintegration of even the utilitarian politics of Cassius. It is not by accident that one of the citizens, inspired by Antony's rhetoric, ambiguously howls "Pluck down forms, windows, any thing" (III.ii.264). Only a scene later, we see just how far all form and humanity have been overthrown:

> *Oct.* Your brother too must die; consent you, Lepidus?
> *Lep.* I do consent,—
> *Oct.*　　　　　　Prick him down, Antony.
> *Lep.* Upon condition Publius shall not live,
> 　　　Who is your sister's son, Mark Antony.
> *Ant.* He shall not live; look, with a spot I damn him.
> 　　　　　　　　　　　　　　　　　(IV.i.2–6)

This is infinitely more horrifying than anything we have seen in the conspiracy, just as the conspiracy itself directly displays a ritual savagery that is infinitely worse than anything Caesar is shown (or even said) to have done in the play. It is this callous playing with the lives of one's blood relatives, as though they were mere counters, that reveals how far Antony has been carried by his contempt for those high motives of Brutus that he had so skillfully turned into their opposites, in his famous funeral oration. If honesty and honor lead to the assassination of one's friends, then moral anarchy can know no limit; so it is in this scene among the members of the new triumvirate. Rome's spiritual disintegration is now complete.

Even in discussing this catastrophe, Brutus shows his customary insensitivity. Thus Messala reports that he has been notified:

> That by proscription and bills of outlawry,
> Octavius, Antony and Lepidus
> Have put to death an hundred senators.
> (IV.iii.173–5)

In the face of this holocaust, Brutus can find nothing more significant to say than:

> Therein our letters do not well agree;
> Mine speak of seventy senators that died.
> (IV.iii.176–7)

He is no more capable of recognizing human suffering as something other than statistics than is Macbeth in his last phases. Like Macbeth, Brutus has been reduced to such insensibility by the consequences of his misjudgments that even the news of his wife's death fails totally to deflect him from the administrative issues that provoke his quarrel with Cassius. In fact, Brutus has become so stupefied that he allows Messala to announce his wife's suicide to him when he already knows of it, and then accepts silently Messala's forced compliment on his impassiveness: "Even so great men great losses must endure" (IV.iii.193). By contrast, the supposedly more corrupt Cassius is shocked by the news of Portia's death, and shaken by the death of even a single senator, Cicero, even though the latter had not been trusted earlier by the conspirators.

Suffering deadens Brutus; by contrast, it strains Cassius' nerves to the breaking point, as his suicide makes clear. The contrast between Cassius' state of mind during the last phases of his career and during the earlier ones is striking. In the beginning, Cassius is contemptuous of the superstitious awe induced in the citizenry by the atmospheric omens of disaster that seem to prefigure the death of Caesar:

For my part, I have walk'd about the streets,
Submitting me unto the perilous night,
And, thus unbraced, Casca, as you see,
Have bared my bosom to the thunder-stone;
And when the cross blue lightning seem'd to open
The breast of heaven, I did present myself
Even in the aim and very flash of it.
(I.iii.46–52)

One feels then that this might indeed be a man to outswim
and even to replace Caesar; but by the end of the play
Cassius has been reduced to the same wavering superstition
that we have already seen in Caesar's response to his wife's
warnings. In telling Messala of the bad omens he has encountered on the way to Philippi, he admits, reluctantly:

You know that I held Epicurus strong
And his opinion: now I change my mind,
And partly credit things that do presage.
(V.i.77–9)

Between the strains of the conspiracy and an increasing
sense of Brutus' ineffective idealism, Cassius crumbles as a
personality, surrendering more and more of the initiative
to Brutus' arbitrary (even if rationalized) acts of will.

Brutus fails altogether to evolve during the action of the
play. To the last he remains convinced, like most dogmatic moralists, that it is the perfection of the will that
constitutes the consummation of all human endeavor:

There is a tide in the affairs of men,
Which, taken at the flood, leads on to fortune;
Omitted, all the voyage of their life
Is bound in shallows and miseries.
On such a full sea are we now afloat;
And we must take the current when it serves,
Or lose our ventures.
(IV.iii.218–24)

Because he interprets all actions in personal philosophical
terms, he acts somewhat at random in political terms—and
almost always prematurely. Thus Antony is astonished by

his opponents' surrender of their strategic mountain vantage-points in the interest merely of precipitating a decision. In this matter, as later in the matter of detailed battle tactics, Cassius is bitterly aware of the justice of Titinius' criticism: "Brutus gave the word too early" (V.iii.5).

There is thus a supreme irony in the last scene of the play, which definitively eliminates the possibility of treating Brutus as a tragic hero, and requires instead that we see the action as a study of political forces. Brutus approaches his own suicide with complacent equanimity, because of his pride in that innocent ability to arouse loyalty that had made him so natural an instrument for conspiracy:

> Countrymen,
> My heart doth joy that yet in all my life
> I found no man but he was true to me.
> I shall have glory by this losing day
> More than Octavius and Mark Antony
> By this vile conquest shall attain unto.
> (V.v.33–8)

This is simply nonsense: Mark Antony not only shook Brutus' blood-stained hand and then went on to betray him, but he will yet become one of the most famous of Roman generals. Similarly, Octavius, as Caesar Augustus, will become not only the most distinguished of Rome's leaders, but also architect of one of the pinnacles of European cultural achievement, celebrated in the poetry of Virgil, Ovid, and Horace. It is this magnificent but unpredictable consummation of a relentless historical progression that Brutus has naively and fatally set himself against.

There is also a final and calculated deflection that is implicit in Shakespeare's assigning the resonant eulogy of the dead Brutus to Antony, who had previously so skillfully discredited the moral status that Brutus had assumed for himself. It may be true that:

> All the conspirators save only he
> Did what they did in envy of great Caesar;
> He only, in general honest thought
> And common good to all, made one of them.
> (V.v.69–72)

Nevertheless, it was Brutus who made the murder feasible by his participation; and, without significantly delaying the empire, he ensured its birth in the midst of even more protracted violence and anarchy than would have been the case if Caesar had lived. Thus, in exaggerating Caesar's loss of flexibility before his death, Shakespeare's intent would appear to be to suggest, not the validity of Brutus' political diagnosis that violence was called for, but the far deeper truth that well-meant violence, even in acute political crisis, only inflames the crisis further. If there is a moral to the play, it is a harsh anticipation of Edith Cavell's severe aphorism: not simply that "Patriotism is not enough," but the even more searching thought: "Sincerity is not enough."

2

ॐ *Coriolanus*

Coriolanus is the last major play of Shakespeare's in which political issues are central both to the action and to the characterization. It is true that Coriolanus displays an eccentric extreme of temperament similar to that shown in *Timon of Athens*, a play in which moral and philosophical values predominate, and we can see in Coriolanus a further step in that investigation of "difficult" personalities which had already presented audiences with *Macbeth* and *Othello*. But while these last-named plays certainly have political overtones (particularly the former), the function of Coriolanus' character is inseparable from the sense of Roman society as a complex and evolving political structure. Although there are full historical foundations in Plutarch for Shakespeare's narrative and for his characterizations in *Coriolanus*, it is clear that it marks the final step in his own investigation of the fateful interaction between private judgment and public values, which had explained the sinister conspiracy of the nobles in *Henry V* through the painful study of Brutus. Brutus, however, has emerged as a paradox: a figure who is both charismatic and, at the same time, unaware both of himself and of the society around him. Coriolanus is both more extreme and more plausible. It is not simply irony that makes this supreme study of heroism come close to being the supreme study in treachery. Shakespeare demonstrates conclusively that individual excellence is at best tangential to political supremacy, and often wholly incompatible with it. Coriolanus is a political disaster for Rome not because, as in the case of Brutus, his virtues are mingled with astounding limitations, but because his absolute integrity and his ruthless directness are both his strength in moments of crisis when the need for them is manifest, and intolerable when peace diminishes the inevitability of their logic. Just as *Othello* displays the moral disaster that inevitably awaits the superman, so *Coriolanus* is a study of his inevitably disastrous political impact.

In many ways Coriolanus, of all Shakespeare's heroes, comes closest to Aristotle's magnanimous man in Book IV of the *Nichomachean Ethics*, "who values himself highly and at the same time justly." Though Aristotle goes on to describe an ideal, it is surprising how many traits correspond to those of Coriolanus:

> he will incur great dangers, and when he does venture he is prodigal of his life as knowing that there are terms on which it is not worth his while to live. He is the sort of man to do kindnesses, but he is ashamed to receive them, the former putting a man in a position of superiority, the latter in that of inferiority; accordingly he will greatly overpay any kindness done to him. . . . Such men seem likewise to remember those they have done kindnesses to, but not those from whom they have received them. . . . Further, it is characteristic of the great-minded man to ask favours not at all, or very reluctantly, but to do a service very readily. . . . It is a property of him also to be open, both in his dislikes and his likings, because concealment is a consequent of fear. Likewise to be careful for reality rather than appearance, and talk and act openly (for his contempt for others makes him a bold man, for which same reason he is apt to speak the truth, except when the principle of reserve comes in).

Scarcely an act of Shakespeare's Coriolanus fails to match this pattern, even down to the wish (I.ix.82ff.) to pay back the hospitality of his poor host, who is among the captives taken by Romans, but whose name the hero cannot remember, once his own "gratitude" has been publicly noted.

Obviously such a man is both an enormous asset to the state in emergencies, and also an enormous provocation to the citizens and democratically elected officials of anything less than a tyranny. A sense of one's own superior wisdom does not make for easy political relationships, and Shakespeare goes out of his way to establish both the transcendent military potency of Coriolanus and the moral and spiritual insignificance of those who understandably but unwisely resent his pride. Yet the crucial difference between the values of Aristotle and Shakespeare appears in the fact that, while the latter recognizes the worth of Coriolanus unreservedly, he also establishes the complete interdependence of that worth and the mediocrity of the average citizen, who lends weight, along with his fellows, to the cutting edge that Coriolanus employs to hew down Rome's enemies. Menenius' fable of the belly and the other organs (I.i.99ff.) displays the interdependence of *all* the parts of the body politic: if the citizenry cannot afford to dispense with the aristocracy, neither can the latter afford to follow the example of Coriolanus and repudiate the former, no matter how justifiably, without thereby fatally rending the fabric of the state.

Furthermore, while the prowess and the merciless realism of Coriolanus are firmly portrayed, the key to his temperament is presented with the bluntness of a case history (which in a political sense this whole play also resembles). It is fatally easy to "pluck out the heart of his mystery," for this is no tragedy of man's most inward intuitions, as is *Hamlet*, but a study of the interaction of simple political forces with conventional excellence. It is no accident that a Freudian approach rationalizes Coriolanus' bizarre consistency of character, just as it debases Hamlet's more elusive subtlety. In one of the earliest speeches of the play, one of the citizens accurately analyzes the motivations of Coriolanus for the "services he has done for his country":

> I say unto you, what he hath done famously, he did it to that end: though soft-conscienced men can be content to say he did it for his country, he did it to please his mother, and to be partly proud; which he is, even to the altitude of his virtue.
>
> (I.i.36–41)

The figure of Volumnia dominates our impression of her son, both here, in his relentless, mother-conditioned pursuit of honor, and later, in his rationalization of his seemingly arbitrary return to loyalty to Rome, when he finally spares the city from destruction at the hands of the army he is leading against those who exiled him from his native land. Coriolanus is obviously mother-fixated to an unusual degree, and we have in Volumnia yet another Shakespearean illustration of the disequilibrium that results from a woman intruding too directly—as Lady Macbeth and Cleopatra do—in affairs that are held to be proper only to men. It is thus surely intended that one be shocked by her quite unfeminine brutality in reproaching the natural apprehensions of her daughter-in-law at the thought of the bloody wounds of Coriolanus:

> Away, you fool! it more becomes a man
> Than gilt his trophy: the breasts of Hecuba,
> When she did suckle Hector, look'd not lovelier
> Than Hector's forehead when it spit forth blood
> At Grecian sword, contemning.
> (I.iii.42–6)

Even the thought of her son's death scarcely affects her: if he had died, "Then his good report should have been my son; I therein would have found issue" (I.iii.22–3). Coriolanus' heroic absolutism thus finds a plausible explanation that is denied us in the comparable case of Hotspur. Shakespeare obviously feels that the overzealous woman both displays, and induces, a too relentless concern with basic issues, which she forces to a solution at any cost. This we see not only in the negative example of Lady Macbeth, but in the worthier, yet no less fatal severity of Desdemona and Cordelia. Coriolanus is no more able to mitigate the indiscreet precision of his judgments than they are; but just as we cannot afford to dismiss the harsh truth of their observations, so we must not only credit Coriolanus with the virtue of accurate observation, we must also recognize that at no point before his exile does he depart from the strict letter of duty and civil obligation. He not only fights magnificently and reproaches his inferiors justly; he also forces himself to meet *all* the conventional requirements for election as consul, with obvious success.

It is clear that Coriolanus' exile results less from his direct provocations, than from the calculated initiatives of those, like the tribunes, whose inadequacy cannot endure the humiliating contrast provided by a hero's mere existence. Nevertheless, it is true that Coriolanus is a scathing critic of the common people. Just before his supreme feat of single-handed invasion of the city of Corioli, Coriolanus blisteringly denounces his timorous Roman troops, who have broken before the enemy's first assault:

> You souls of geese,
> That bear the shapes of men, how have you run
> From slaves that apes would beat! Pluto and hell!
> All hurt behind; backs red, and faces pale
> With flight and agued fear! Mend and charge home,
> Or, by the fires of heaven, I'll leave the foe
> And make my wars on you.
> (I.iv.34–40)

The bitter threat is obviously not accidental, prefiguring as it does the ultimate result of his exile. This is imposed through the exploitation (by the shoddier elements in the Roman state) of the popular resentment at such legitimate reproaches. It is in this censorious frame of mind that Coriolanus also reacts to the enhancement of democratic representation in the Roman constitution, by the creation of popularly elected tribunes, or magistrates:

> The common file—a plague! tribunes for them!—
> The mouse ne'er shunn'd the cat as they did budge
> From rascals worse than they.
> (I.vi.43–5)

Yet, under the inspiration of his example, the Roman troops universally rally in the battle at Corioli where he earns his name, and win the compliment of their leader: "which of you / But is four Volsces" (I.vi.77–8). Coriolanus can be frank in praise as well as censure. Nor does he have an exaggerated sense of his own worth, as the citizens often imply. He sees it for what it is: by the highest standards, only what *every* citizen owes to the state. Thus he refuses any unusual reward in good faith, allying himself, like Henry V at Agincourt, with all who have fought with him against the common enemy:

> I thank you, general;
> But cannot make my heart consent to take
> A bribe to pay my sword: I do refuse it;
> And stand upon my common part with those
> That have beheld the doing.
> (I.ix.36–40)

He thus requires of himself no less than he exacts of others, and if he has a fault it is only that of rather naively measuring others against what he frequently announces to be his own routine virtues. He is merely the good citizen in his own eyes; anyone doing less is properly censured, while he himself expects no unusual praise or reward for fulfilling his obligations. What we have in this play then is the confrontation of the mediocre by the true norm of civic responsibility. Its repudiation by the masses is a kind of political analogue to the crucifixion of Christ as a criminal; for, as we have noted, never until the climactic monstrosity of his exile does Coriolanus effectively fail in the visible discharge of his political obligations.

It is not by accident that two anonymous officers of the

Roman state debate the issues and reluctantly conclude that Coriolanus cannot properly be censured for his lack of diplomacy. There is choric force in their final judgment of his status:

> He hath deserved worthily of his country: and his ascent is not by such easy degrees as those who, having been supple and courteous to the people, bonneted, without any further deed to have them at all into their estimation and report: but he hath so planted his honours in their eyes, and his actions in their hearts, that for their tongues to be silent, and not confess so much, were a kind of ingrateful injury; to report otherwise, were a malice, that giving itself the lie, would pluck reproof and rebuke from every ear that heard it.
>
> (II.ii.27–38)

This is the political situation that Shakespeare has worked to establish: the confrontation of political institutions by a hero of undisguised virtue, a Henry V without cunning. The story of their interaction displays the inadequacy of the purely ethical view of politics that was taken by the *Mirrors for Magistrates,* with which the sixteenth century had attempted to vindicate the correlation between the failure of a ruler and his disregard of Christian ethics. Coriolanus seems to initially lack the Christian virtue of mercifulness (though even this he ultimately acquires), but he transgresses against few other premises of excellence in such moralizing historians as Hall: he is deliberately made a kind of classical Henry V in all but that guilefulness in which Shakespeare suggests that the Lancastrian kings anticipated Machiavelli. Shakespeare is thus able to demonstrate plausibly that unqualified virtue is not able to function in a normal political environment. Without his guile, Shakespeare implies, Henry V would readily have fallen into conspiracies himself, as his father had always anticipated that he would (*1HIV,* III.ii.122ff.).

Nor does Shakespeare allow us any simple escape from this sinister demonstration that your innocent man is your best traitor. It is true that Coriolanus' ultimate ambition

for the consulship results from his unwise assent to the
full extravagance of his mother's aspirations:

> I have lived
> To see inherited my very wishes
> And the buildings of my fancy: only
> There's one thing wanting, which I doubt not but
> Our Rome will cast upon thee.
> (II.i.214–18)

Coriolanus' own good sense somewhat drily points up the
difficulty that seeking the supreme political office will
present for him:

> Know, good mother,
> I had rather be their servant in my way
> Than sway with them in theirs.
> (II.i.218–20)

But it will not serve to quote some of Coriolanus' later
speeches in order to prove that he is unworthy of such
political office because of that gross contempt for the
citizenry which he ultimately extends to censure of the
democratically amended constitution. The fact that he has,
with whatever bad grace, undergone the full rigor of
popular solicitation of votes and legally secured election,
is formally established by Menenius:

> You have stood your limitation; and the tribunes
> Endue you with the people's voice: remains
> That, in the official marks invested, you
> Anon do meet the senate.
> (II.iii.146–9)

It is the unjust attempt of the envious tribunes to revoke
this concluded election (II.iii.225ff.) that alone launches
Coriolanus onto a denunciation of the political situation:

> This double worship
> Where one part does disdain with cause, the other
> Insult without all reason, where gentry, title, wisdom,
> Cannot conclude but by the yea and no
> Of general ignorance,—it must omit

Real necessities, and give way the while
To unstable slightness: purpose so barr'd, it follows
Nothing is done to purpose.
                    (III.i.142–9)

He derives from this understandable judgment the inex-
pedient conclusion that the office of popularly elected
tribune should be discontinued. The tribunes' flagrant
abuse of authority in recalling the consular election, while
it justifies his immediate personal reaction, does not necessarily justify the broader political conclusions he draws
from it. Volumnia is right to reproach him only for sacrificing the ultimate authority of the consulship merely to
indulge in local resentments, however natural:

                    You are too absolute;
Though therein you can never be too noble,
But when extremities speak. I have heard you say,
Honour and policy, like unsever'd friends,
I' the war do grow together: grant that, and tell me,
In peace what each of them by other lose,
That they combine not here.
                    (III.ii.39–45)

The admonition is just—and it is significant that Volumnia is already losing the initiative. It is no longer the
sanction of her own ambition that she invokes, but the
precision of Coriolanus' own best judgments. Once again,
Coriolanus proves ultimately amenable to good sense:
despite his disgust at the "harlot's spirit" required
(III.ii.112), he undertakes to adjust himself to the requirements of the political situation without any reservation or
hesitation: "the word is 'mildly.'" (III.ii.142) It is only
the willful malice of the tribunes that could cause him to
break this promise, and it is hard to see how he could
avoid resentment at the charge of being "a traitor to the
people" (III.iii.66), in view of the near-fatal risks he has
so recently borne in Rome's service. Indeed, to endure
the charge would be almost as dangerous as to denounce
it. It is apparent that we have here the political equivalent

of Cordelia's ethical dilemma in the face of Lear's invitation to participate in her sisters' dishonest and mercenary protestations of filial devotion. The real traitors to Rome are, of course, the tribunes who (unlike Coriolanus) *have* violated the constitution; but by the viciousness implicit in this very act they are enabled without a qualm to slander with the name of their own guilt anyone whose position threatens theirs.

Strict virtue is shown to be immediately powerless in such a situation, though it is not ultimately so—for both Cordelia and Coriolanus lead an enemy army against the homeland whose magistrates have insisted on labeling them as traitors before the event. Their accusers thus almost succeed in bringing the initially false identification to the point of realization. If one is already treated as criminal, it is the rare spirit indeed that will not ultimately live up to the charge, as Shakespeare himself observed ruefully:

> 'Tis better to be vile than vile esteem'd,
> When not to be receives reproach of being,
> And the just pleasure lost which is so deem'd
> Not by our feeling but by others' seeing.
> *(Sonnet 121, 1–4)*

The only effective way to meet the insidious designs of the corrupt politician at the moment of crisis is thus to duplicate them, and this Coriolanus scrupulously refuses to do in any real sense. It is in this spirit of integrity that he reverses the tribunes' sentence of exile in the paradoxical assertion to the mob, "I banish you" (III.iii.123). In a very definite sense, he is the true spirit of Rome, and where he is, civic virtue is—thus, the people he leaves are really being separated from their own true state, and, as he says, "I shall be loved when I am lack'd" (IV.i.15)— just as Cordelia is.

One cannot see how Coriolanus could have behaved otherwise without dishonesty. The political syllogism is as complete and inescapable as the ethical dilemma that confronts Cordelia in defining the relationship between a

loving father and a marriageable daughter. Menenius'
rueful comment on Coriolanus is true of Cordelia as well:
"His nature is too noble for the world" (III.i.255). In
order to avoid simplifications of this almost irresolvable
tension, Shakespeare is careful to define the elements of
his argument early in *Coriolanus*. On the one hand, a
citizen firmly establishes the real status of the electoral
power to deny the consulship that is vested in the
populace:

> We have power in ourselves to do it, but it is a power
> that we have no power to do; for if he show us his
> wounds and tell us his deeds, we are to put our tongues
> into those wounds and speak for them; so, if he tells us
> his noble deeds, we must also tell him our noble ac-
> ceptance of them. Ingratitude is monstrous, and for the
> multitude to be ingrateful, were to make a monster of
> the multitude; of the which we being members, should
> bring ourselves to be monstrous members.
>
> (II.iii.4–13)

The withdrawal of the affirmed vote is thus a monstrous
act in the very terms proposed by the play, nor do
Coriolanus' sentiments justify it, even though they are
couched in terms directly contrary to those of the citizen's
speech above:

> Better it is to die, better to starve,
> Than crave the hire which first we do deserve.
> Why in this woolvish toge should I stand here,
> To beg of Hob and Dick, that do appear,
> Their needless vouches? Custom calls me to't:
> What custom wills, in all things should we do't,
> The dust on antique time would lie unswept
> And mountainous error be too highly heapt
> For truth to o'er-peer. Rather than fool it so,
> Let the high office and the honour go
> To one that would do thus. I am half through;
> The one part suffer'd, the other will I do.
>
> (II.iii.120–31)

There is an interesting contrast between the citizens' speciousness, and the surly assent to duty of Coriolanus' last line and a half. Shakespeare's presentation of the two patterns provides an analogy to the parable of the Two Sons (Matthew, 21:28-32). There is no doubt who here corresponds to the son who accepts his father's orders as legitimate and then fails to abide by them, and who matches the son that denounces the orders but finally obeys them. Offensive as his speech may be to democrats and constitutionalists, Coriolanus is surly but honest; more important, he proves invariably law-abiding in the long run, however unlikely this may appear, as, for example, when he is about to lead Rome's enemies into the city.

We sympathize with the citizen of whom Coriolanus crudely inquires, "I pray, your price o'the consulship?" only to get the modest reply: "The price is to ask it kindly" (II.iii.81). Improbably enough, Coriolanus finally agrees to do just that, although with a witty minimum of insincerity:

> I will, sir, flatter my sworn brother, the people, to earn a dearer estimation of them; 'tis a condition they account gentle: and since the wisdom of their choice is rather to have my hat than my heart, I will practise the insinuating nod and be off to them most counterfeitly; that is, sir, I will counterfeit the bewitchment of some popular man and give it bountiful to the desirers. Therefore, beseech you, I may be consul.
>
> (II.iii.101-10)

It is a brilliantly ironic but scarcely dishonest performance, for once neatly designed to appear gracious yet not to disavow the speaker's contempt for solicited popularity. It cleverly states the issue in a form that is true to the speaker's belief yet inaccessible to the careless audience of citizens, who at once, symbolically, commit themselves to Coriolanus, a man who here really despises them. This is a neat validation of Coriolanus' argument against the judgment of the crowd, and the ambivalence of its usual heroes. Only a man who thus covertly despises the mob can rule it. However, for all his open contempt for the new constitution, the more carefully one examines the actual behavior of Coriolanus, the harder it is to show that he is guilty of any failure to observe the law before his exile. He merely *says* shocking and ungracious things; but it is a pitiful charge against a man to say that he has intolerant opinions or mother-induced motives, if all his *acts* reveal a genuine submission to the will of the majority. If we bear this in mind, it must seem strange to make his final mercy to Rome such a theme for contemptuous criticism as it often is.

We are now in a position to resolve such problems of characterization, and the political issues raised by the last two acts of the play, acts in which Coriolanus appears to behave in a way—both traitorous and vacillating—that belies the substantial integrity of his previous behavior. There is no doubt that for a time the simpler Coriolanus surrenders to that instinct for revenge that Hamlet is subtle enough to resist from the start, even though the admonition of his father's ghost is at least as compelling an incentive as the Roman evaluation of Coriolanus as a confirmed traitor. In his overprompt reaction, Coriolanus thus makes the same mistake as Othello, confounding understandable private resentment with an objective justification for harsh punishment of the offender. As a result, Coriolanus is rapidly betrayed into the same kind of appalling dilemma as faced Macbeth: he cannot either proceed or abandon his assault on Rome, without betraying himself: "Returning were as tedious as go o'er."

The bitter irony of Coriolanus' last campaign is that he cannot win it—as his mother, reduced at last to mere wisdom, lucidly points out:

> Thou know'st, great son,
> The end of war's uncertain, but this is certain,
> That, if thou conquer Rome, the benefit
> Which thou shalt thereby reap is such a name,

Whose reputation shall be dogg'd with curses,
Whose chronicle thus writ: 'The man was noble,
But with his last attempt he wiped it out;
Destroy'd his country, and his name remains
To the ensuing age abhorr'd.'
(V.iii.140–8)

The only conceivable alternative to this, as she plausibly
represents it, is that:

                    . . . thou
Must, as a foreign recreant, be led
With manacles through our streets.
(V.iii.113–15)

It is this pair of equally impossible alternatives that accounts for the otherwise implausible surrender of command of the Coriolian army to Coriolanus by his bitterest
enemy, Aufidius. The Coriolian perceives the ultimate impossibility of Coriolanus' position and is therefore content
to give way to him, because:

When, Caius, Rome is thine,
Thou art poor'st of all; then shortly art thou mine.
(IV.vii.56–7)

In contemplating the solution to the dilemma achieved
by Coriolanus, we must note how the whole situation
irresistibly frames itself in Christian terms, which proved
far less relevant to *Julius Caesar*. It appears that, the more
deeply Shakespeare saturates himself in the politics of
pagan Rome, the more inescapable become the terms of
reference proposed to him by the New Testament. Thus,
when Cominius reports the terms of Coriolanus' refusal
of his pleas, he unmistakably reverses Christ's parable of
the weeds in the wheat (Matthew, 13:24–30):

I offer'd to awaken his regard
For's private friends: his answer to me was,
He could not stay to pick them in a pile
Of noisome musty chaff: he said 'twas folly,

For one poor grain or two, to leave unburnt,
And still to nose the offence.
(V.i.23-8)

The contrast with even the less liberal spirit of the Old
Testament is conspicuous: Abraham's negotiations with
God to spare Sodom (Genesis, 18:23-32) ultimately secure
the agreement that the city will be spared if a mere ten
of its citizens prove virtuous. The fiercer severity of
Coriolanus is testimony to his nearly diabolical resentment.
Cominius rightly presents him as a kind of pathological
case: "He was a kind of nothing" (V.i.13). Coriolanus has
become, as the result of his monstrous treatment, un-
amenable to traditional terms:

He is their god: he leads them like a thing
Made by some other deity than nature.
(IV.vi.90-1)

As long as Coriolanus remains in this non-human state of
mind, Rome is doomed by the results of its own actions.
Menenius can do no more than ruefully anticipate the
terms of Christianity, as the Romans' only (and, unlikely)
hope:

We are all undone, unless
The noble man have mercy.
(IV.vi.107-8)

How paradoxical such an act must appear in a pagan context is suggested when Aufidius begins to realize that it
is toward this course that Coriolanus is directing himself:

I am glad thou hast set thy mercy and thy honour
At difference in thee: out of that I'll work
Myself a former fortune.
(V.iii.199-201)

To Aufidius, it is a dangerous weakness that one's personal
honor (and well-being) should be subject to a higher and
often conflicting order of values, which might be deliberately preferred.

As for Coriolanus, what makes him conscious of this higher order is, of course, the self-abasement of his once lordly mother. He suddenly realizes that, if any order is to be maintained in the world, it must be at the price of surrendering the inflexible application of principle, which otherwise will end by turning the world upside-down:

> What is this:
> Your knees to me? to your corrected son?
> Then let the pebbles on the hungry beach
> Fillip the stars; then let the mutinous winds
> Strike the proud cedars 'gainst the fiery sun;
> Murdering impossibility, to make
> What cannot be, slight work.
> (V.iii.56–62)

The son recognizes that his mother's gesture of humility is an example to him, in his relation to his erring motherland, for which she is a kind of figure at this point. Unlike Lear or Macbeth, Coriolanus does not allow his resentment against the fallibility of the world to commit him even temporarily to a nihilistic delight in universal disorder. Exactly as he has earlier stopped short of the brink of anarchic individualism, just when it had seemed that his ideas must commit him to unqualified action against the state's traditional forms, so now he subjects his instincts and his judgment to an intuition of a higher order of behavior, which preserves the state even while he is suffering from its deficiencies. He now consciously assents to that deep humility in the face of his wrongs which he had hitherto affected resentfully from time to time through mere policy, or outside pressure. Like Hamlet, Coriolanus ends by understanding and thus mastering his predicament.

The solution of his dilemma that is arrived at by Coriolanus is at the same time adequate, paradoxical, and personally fatal:

> Behold, the heavens do ope,
> The gods look down, and this unnatural scene
> They laugh at. O my mother, mother! O!

You have won a happy victory to Rome;
But, for your son,—believe it, O, believe it,
Most dangerously you have with him prevail'd,
If not most mortal to him. But, let it come.
Aufidius, though I cannot make true wars,
I'll frame convenient peace.
                    (V.iii.183–91)

The speech reflects a fascinating evolution of personality in that the dashing, bellicose young leader of the first act, ever spoiling for a fight, has now evolved into a peacemaker whose personal honor and very life is to be laid down in the interest of peace, "a man by his own alms empoison'd,/And with his charity slain" (V.vi.11–12). And it must be pointed out that the terms of the treaty are in fact happy for all parties: the sack of Rome has been averted, but the Coriolian army returns home laden with spoils, and with more advantage over Rome than they had ever hoped for in the past. Aufidius is able to alienate his compatriots from Coriolanus only by preventing the terms of the treaty from being publicly proclaimed. The play thus ends on a final note of irony: Coriolanus has won for Corioli as much by peaceful methods as he had won for Rome by war—and in each case he is ultimately rewarded by bitter popular hatred. Rome, under the influence of the tribunes, execrated and exiled him; Corioli, through a similar conspiracy led by Aufidius, also turns against him, and assassinates the worthiest man among them. It thus appears that the mob cannot be governed by the purely virtuous, in either state.

Plutarch drily notes that the Coriolians paid for their folly far more dearly than did the Romans. Once Coriolanus had been murdered, the Roman resurgence began, and "the whole state of the Volsces heartily wished him alive again." Finally "the Romans overcame them in battle, in which [Aufidius] was slain in the field, and the flower of all their force was put to the sword; so that they were compelled to accept most shameful conditions of peace." Shakespeare shows us none of this, except to display the

Coriolians' crude misunderstanding of the last phase of Coriolanus' career:

> His own impatience
> Takes from Aufidius a great part of the blame.
> Let's make the best of it.
> (V.vi.146-8)

Obviously Shakespeare has little hope of an advance or even a variation in political awareness as a result of Coriolanus' career. Yet the truth remains that Coriolanus' conduct has been a salutary example of how—even by audiences, and by generations of critics like ourselves— facts are often forgotten, so that the best may readily appear the worst. More positively, the play shows how an attempt at the greatest wrong may lead to awareness of the highest good.

Perhaps Shakespeare was also not unaware of the theme's relevance to the execution of Essex, the friend of his patron, for similarly challenging the established order. Unfortunately, Essex had few of Coriolanus' moral virtues and most of his political defects, so that his career could never stand as an epitome of the irresolvable tension between the virtues that vindicate a leader and the dubious skills by which he necessarily maintains his authority. In *Coriolanus* Shakespeare convinced himself that these opposites could *not* be reconciled; thereafter, he concerned himself chiefly with man as a complex individual primarily learning how to manage his personal relationships—often at the cost of political success. In a sense, our own responses to Coriolanus suggest why politics no longer seems worthy of interest to Shakespeare. He demonstrates that, in political affairs, men are not meaningfully interested in what others really do, but only in what they seem to be. Coriolanus is thus the great corollary of Milton's Satan: Satan appears truly heroic, yet acts with uniform destructiveness; Coriolanus perpetually appears intolerable to us, yet always acts for the best. Both are studies addressed to the purging of misjudgment from their audiences. Looking back over the similar reversals of our expectations revealed in our study of earlier Shakespearean characters, like Henry V and Brutus, we may well conclude that it is indeed just this kind of challenge to simplifying political judgments which constitutes the distinctive cathartic function of Shakespeare's political plays.

FURTHER READING

THE HISTORY plays of Shakespeare are treated incidentally in many of the broader studies of his work, which are too numerous to be listed here, and there are also many specialized essays and articles about individual problems and plays. For the fullest information about Shakespearean studies one can consult *A Shakespeare Bibliography (to 1930)*, edited by W. Ebisch, with L. L. Schücking (Oxford: Clarendon Press, 1931), *Supplement 1930-35* (Oxford: Clarendon Press, 1937); *A Classified Shakespeare Bibliography 1936-58*, edited by G. R. Smith (University Park: Pennsylvania State University Press, 1963); and for recent work, the bibliography published every year in the May issue of *PMLA*.

The most fully annotated edition of the plays in single volumes is the *New Variorum*, edited by H. H. Furness, et al. (New York: J. B. Lippincott & Co., 1871-); but a very useful modern edition is the new *Arden*, now published jointly by Harvard and Methuen. G. L. Kittredge has helpfully annotated some plays now published in single play editions (Boston: Ginn and Co., 1957); and J. D. Wilson has freshly edited the whole series in the *New Shakespeare* (Cambridge: Cambridge University Press, 1921-). All these single play texts are beginning to appear in paperback, as are many of the other texts mentioned below.

Though it is somewhat dated, the best source for facts

about Shakespeare probably remains E. K. Chambers, *William Shakespeare: A Study of Facts and Problems*, 2 vols. (Oxford: Clarendon Press, 1930). The fullest collection of Shakespeare's sources is *Narrative and Dramatic Sources of Shakespeare*, edited by G. Bullough (New York: Columbia University Press, 1957–); but handier volumes are *Holinshed's Chronicles as Used in Shakespeare's Plays*, edited by A. and J. Nicoll (London: Everyman, 1927), and *Shakespeare's Plutarch*, edited by T. J. B. Spencer (Baltimore: Penguin, 1964). The following are some of the most useful books which have dealt primarily or largely with the history plays in more recent years: P. Alexander, *Shakespeare's Henry VI and Richard III* (Cambridge: Cambridge University Press, 1929); C. L. Barber, *Shakespeare's Festive Comedy* (Princeton: Princeton University Press, 1959), for Falstaff; L. B. Campbell, *Shakespeare's "Histories": Mirrors of Elizabethan Policy* (San Marino: Huntingdon Library, 1947); H. B. Charlton, *Shakespeare, Politics and Politicians* (Oxford: Clarendon Press, 1929); M. Charney, editor, *Discussions of Shakespeare's Roman Plays* (Boston: D. C. Heath & Co., 1964); R. J. Dorius, editor, *Discussions of Shakespeare's Histories* (Boston: D. C. Heath & Co., 1964); J. Palmer, *Political Characters in Shakespeare* (New York: Macmillan & Co., 1945); M. M. Reese, *The Cease of Majesty* (London: E. Arnold, Ltd., 1961); I. Ribner, *The English History Play in the Age of Shakespeare* (Princeton: Princeton University Press, 1957); S. C. Sen Gupta, *Shakespeare's History Plays* (Oxford: Clarendon Press, 1965); E. M. W. Tillyard, *Shakespeare's History Plays* (London: Chatto & Windus, 1944); D. A. Traversi, *Shakespeare from Richard II to Henry IV* (Stanford: Stanford University Press, 1957), and *Shakespeare: the Roman Plays* (Stanford: Stanford University Press, 1963); J. D. Wilson, *The Fortunes of Falstaff* (Cambridge: Cambridge University Press, 1943). Other studies of the history plays have been surveyed by H. Jenkins, "Shakespeare's History Plays: 1900–1951," *Shakespeare Survey*, VI (1953), 1–15.

INDEX

STUDIES IN LANGUAGE
AND LITERATURE